MW00987226

Sea Stories

True Adventures of Great Lakes Freighter Captain, Richard Metz

by Richard Metz

Adventure Publications
Cambridge, Minnesota

DEDICATION

I dedicate this book to the hundreds of seamen who were lost at sea and never made it back to shore and who are entombed and still standing their watch aboard their ships.

ACKNOWLEDGMENTS

I want to give thanks for my oldest friend, Vince Jordan, who got me interested in the boats; how he loaned me one hundred dollars to go to Duluth to get my first deckhand job on the S.S. *Thomas Wilson*. Years ago Vince taught me how to scuba dive. Without his teaching I probably would not have been a shipwreck diver or have written two books on diving and sailing the Great Lakes.

Thanks, Vince.

I also would like to give special thanks to one of my best friends, the late Stewart F. Belanger, who years ago encouraged me to write a book about my experiences at sea. Year after year when I came home from the lakes I would tell Stewart my sea stories. Year after year he would tell me to put my stories into book form. Thanks, Stewart, wherever you are.

Captain Richard D. Metz, 2017

Back cover photo courtesy of Boatnerd (www.boatnerd.com), photo of Captain Metz courtesy of Richard Metz

Photo credits listed on each image.

Cover and book design by Lora Westberg

10 9 8 7 6 5 4 3 2 1

Copyright 2017 by Richard Metz
Published by Adventure Publications
An imprint of AdventureKEEN
820 Cleveland Street South
Cambridge, Minnesota 55008
(800) 678-7006
www.adventurepublications.net
All rights reserved
Printed in China

ISBN: 978-1-59193-639-8; eISBN: 978-1-59193-760-9

TABLE OF CONTENTS

HOW IT USED TO BE

I started my sailing career on April 27, 1964—53 years ago. I started as an ordinary seaman aboard the *Thomas Wilson*. I retired in 1999 and am in my 80s now. There are not too many of us old guys around anymore.

The captains of today, with their 1000-footers and powerful diesel engines, have no idea what it was like in the 1960s. They will never experience any of the following:

- Sailing a ship that was built at the turn of the century, and ships that were only 500 or 620 feet long

- The labor involved in securing 35 telescopic sliding hatches, which were sealed with tarps, often frozen, and had to be wrestled into place by strong backs and batten boards

- Sailing aboard a ship with a steam engine powered by coal; a top speed of 8 knots with fly ash spewing all over the deck

- The thrill of being in a gale with the pilothouse forward and the bow hitting a high wave head-on; or the feeling of the bow going down into the trough of a wave and having the stern come entirely out of the water, the prop shaking the whole ship causing the engineer to cut the speed down; then, when the stern settled, giving the ship full steam ahead, so the bow would come up, plowing a wall of water over the pilothouse, a small heater in the front window the only thing preventing the window from freezing up

- In those days, there were no interior tunnels if you wanted to move through the ship during a storm; instead, there was a wire cable strung on the deck and leading from the pilot-house to the cabins; hooking up to the cable was the only way to ensure you wouldn't get washed off the deck

- The galley served fine food, including homemade bread, rolls, pie, and steak that was 1½ inch thick

- The skipper had an old RCA radar and only used it in fog, but it was not very good, it took several minutes to make one complete sweep and by that time the target had disappeared until the next sweep; if you wanted to find a ship's position, there was no GPS, you had to use radio direction finding

- Weather forecasts were announced twice daily at 0700 and 1900 hours on AM radios; now we get weather 24 hours a day, and it is far more accurate

- At the Soo Locks, we used all four locks and sometimes the Canadian Lock. Many times, we had to reduce our speed or anchor because of all the traffic. Once in the lock vendors with bikes used to come alongside of the ship selling papers, tobacco, and candy; not any more

- I used to climb up the forward or aft mast to change light bulbs, and in freezing weather climb up the rear ladder on the pilothouse to chip away ice so the radar scanner would rotate; there were no bow thrusters or twin screws to help with shiphandling, we had anchors and know-how

I am glad to have sailed the way we used to do it, but I would not mind going for a trip on a thousand-footer and seeing all of the new things they have today.

CANADA

Thunder Bay

PASSAGE ISLAND
LIGHTHOUSE

BLAKE POINT
LIGHT

Lake
Superior

Ontario

Minnesota

MINNESOTA'S
NORTH SHORE

ROCK OF AGES
LIGHTHOUSE

Copper Harbor

Silver Bay

Houghton

STANNARD ROCK
LIGHTHOUSE

DEVILS ISLAND
LIGHTHOUSE

Two Harbors

KEEWEENAW
PENINSULA

Keeweenaw Waterway

Sault Ste. Marie

Duluth

Marquette

MacArthur and Poe Locks

Superior

Michigan

Straits of
Mackinac

Port Dolomite

Mackinaw City

Calcite

Stonepo

Alpena

Green
Bay

Traverse City

Manistee

Wisconsin

Bay City

Lake
Michigan

Michigan

Milwaukee

Holland

Iowa

Toledo

Chicago

Indiana Harbor

Burns Harbor

Gary

Illinois

Indiana

6

To the Atlantic Ocean ⟶

Quebec

Saint Lawrence
River

South Shore Canal
● St. Lambert Lock

Montreal ●
Beauharnois Locks ●● Cote Ste.
Catherine Lock

Vermon

Eisenhower Lock ●
Snell Lock ●
Iroquois Lock ●

Lake
Champlain

Georgian
Bay

Ontario

**Lake
Huron**

● Owen Sound

**Lake
Ontario**

Toronto ●

New York

Ma

● Goderich

Hamilton ●
Thorold ●
Port Colborne ●

● Buffalo

Welland Canal
(and locks)

Co

Port Huron
● Sarnia
St. Clair River

Lake St. Clair
etroit
● Windsor

**Lake
Erie**

● Conneaut
Ashtabula ●

● SOUTHEAST
SHOAL

● Cleveland

New
Jersey

Pennsylvania

Ohio

Maryland

Delaware

West Virginia

Virginia

7

The *Thomas Wilson*; taken by Dick Metz

GREENHORN

Ship: *Thomas Wilson*
Rank: Deckhand
Year: 1964

One night as I sat on a roll of paper during a break at my job at the paper mill, I was thinking about the lake—Lake Superior—and I drew my thoughts on the paper. It was a large drawing of the lake, its islands, shipwreck locations, and the shipping routes from Duluth to the Soo Locks in Sault Ste. Marie, Michigan.

A coworker walked by and looked at my drawing. "That's very good," he said. "Could I have it?" I tore off the piece of paper and handed it to him.

"Dick, you love the lakes so much, why don't you quit and get a job on the boats?"

I thought about this for a few days and made up my mind. When I asked the foreman if I could have a few days off, he said, "Yes, but for what?"

"To try to find out how to get a job on the boats."

"Go ahead." He understood my feelings. "I know your heart is set on the boats and not on this job."

Starting Out

I drove up to Duluth and registered with Mike Ross at the Lake Carriers' Association Hiring Hall. "Do you want to work in the engine room or as a deckhand?" he asked.

"What's the difference?" I had no idea.

Mike explained each job to me. When he finished, I didn't hesitate. I did not want to work where it was so hot, and I wanted to see where I was going. "I want to be a deckhand," I said.

I drove back home, quit the mill, and packed my seabag.

About a week later, Mike called. "I've got a deckhand job that opened up on the *Thomas F. Cole* for United States Steel. Come on in to my office and I'll get you set up."

My friends gave me a going-away party. Big mistake; they should have had it without me. When I arrived at Mike's office, he took one look at me and said, "What happened to you? Don't you know you have to take a physical for this company?"

"No, I didn't know." Ashamed, I went off to get my physical. I failed it, due to an elevated blood sugar level, an elevated heart rate and high blood pressure (otherwise known as a hangover).

I went aboard the anyway and asked for the Captain. A crewman led me to his quarters. We exchanged introductions, and the Captain sat down. I figured that since he sat down, it was okay for me to sit, too. When I did, there was a crunching noise. I moved to locate the source of the crunch, and discovered that I had sat on his glasses. "Things are off to a bad start," I said to myself.

I told the Captain my story. "I'm not a drinker," I said, "and I would like to work on your boat."

"You look big and strong, and I'd like to have you as a deckhand," he replied. "But it's company policy that if you don't pass a physical, you don't get the job."

That was that. I went back to Mike's office and told him what happened. "Well, there are no more jobs on the board," he said. "If you want to go back home, I will contact you if another ship becomes available."

Waiting It Out

Instinct told me differently. I knew he wouldn't call me. I had had my chance to sail, and I goofed up the opportunity. I decided to sit at the Lake Carriers' hall every day until a ship came in needing a deckhand. For two weeks, I sat in the hall from 0800 to 1600 and played checkers every day. I became so good at checkers that I beat everyone in the hall and no one would play against me anymore. Ship came; ships left. Jobs were filled, but there were none for me.

Finally, Mike said that I could have a job on the steamer *Thomas Wilson*. I was to meet the ship at Silver Bay, Minnesota, in two days. Mike's advice: "No partying!"

I drove to Silver Bay and got a hotel room. The night before the Wilson was due to arrive, I walked down to the cliffs that overlooked the lake, and I stared out across Lake Superior.

"What's in it for me?" I wondered. "What will tomorrow bring?"

I was a bit nervous. I watched a freighter pass by very slowly. All of her deck lights and navigation lights shone brightly, and I heard the banging of the hatch covers as they were being lifted off the hatches. The ship was headed for the loading berth at Silver Bay. I went back to my hotel and tried to sleep.

Next to the Thomas Wilson

My friend Vince had sailed on the lakes for a while, and I thought about what he had told me about sailing. He said to bring my diving gear, because if the ship sinks, I would survive. Vince had said it was important to batten down the hatches and make sure they were down tight.

Vince also gave me some advice to help me get along with the crew. He said that when he went into the mess hall to eat, he looked around the table and saw a few empty stools, so he sat down on one. A big, mean-looking sailor came in and saw Vince sitting on his stool. Without a word, he smacked Vince alongside the head. Vince landed on the deck. He warned me to ask where my seat was located when I went into the mess hall. Vince told me that beginning on August 1 of each year, the ships do not go more than a mile from the shore because the lakes get too rough, and it is dangerous.

With my head full of all these thoughts, I finally fell into an uneasy sleep. Early the next morning, I went for breakfast and then drove to the Silver Bay pellet plant. I parked my car behind the guard shack at the entrance. "I'm here to go aboard the *Wilson* as deckhand," I told the guard. After he made a few phone calls, a truck pulled up in front of the shack, and I loaded my gear on it. The driver took me to the dock where the *Wilson* was loading iron ore (taconite) pellets.

My mouth fell open when I first saw the *Wilson*. God, she was big! She had a huge black hull and a black smokestack with a large white "W" painted on it. The truck driver pulled up to the boarding ladder. I got out, looked up, and saw two men standing on deck with a line. One yelled, "Tie your seabag with this line and we'll bring it aboard!"

I remembered something Vince had told me. "Don't trust anyone aboard a ship; they will steal anything." I tied that line to my seabag and raced up the ladder to keep an eye on my bag.

Halfway up the ladder, I heard the seaman say, "What have you got in this seabag?"

"Just my gear." Little did he know, my gear included a diving tank, wet suit, mask, fins, and an 18-pound weight belt!

I threw the bag over my shoulder, and he picked up my other smaller, lighter bag. He took me forward to show me my quarters. "Get yourself settled, and then report to the mate on deck," he instructed.

About midship was a man with a pen and paper in hand. I figured that he had to be the mate. I went up to him and introduced myself, saying that I was the new deckhand and this was my first time on a ship. I was really a greenhorn.

He turned, shook my hand, and said, "That's the way I like them. Then I can train a man my way."

"What should I do?" I asked.

"Stand by."

I looked around the deck. "Stand by what?" I asked.

The mate looked at me. "Boy, I guess you are a greenhorn. It's dinnertime, so go to the galley and have your dinner."

As I headed for the galley, I saw Vince's face in my mind. "Watch where you sit. Remember that big guy!" I told myself. I opened the door to the mess hall, stepped inside, and met the porter, Ernie. "I'm the new deckhand," I announced. "Where should I sit?"

"Anyplace you like is fine."

I chose the very last stool, thinking no one would want that spot and I could keep my eye out for the big guy.

Ernie served me a big T-bone and baked potatoes with homemade buns. Other crewmembers came in to eat, and soon the table was full. They all shook hands with me and were very friendly. There was no big, mean guy.

Battening Down the Hatches

Dinner done, I went back out on deck. "Put on the hatches and all the clamps," the mate instructed.

After the first hatch was on, I began tightening down the clamps, and again, I thought about what Vince had said. "Make sure they are on tight!" I found a small length of pipe, which gave me more leverage, and I really tightened each clamp down. I had tightened the clamps on about four hatches, when I heard loud voices. Steam winches were clanking, and soon men were climbing up the ladder from the dock as fast as they could.

I was watching all the commotion when the ship's whistle blew. It scared the heck right out of me, and I jumped about a foot off the deck. I quickly learned that when a ship was leaving port, the whistle was sounded to alert other ships that one was leaving the dock. I felt slight motion and saw the dock moving slowly away from the side of the ship. A strange feeling came over me, and I felt like jumping off the ship back onto the dock, heading for my car, and driving back home.

The daydream ended abruptly when the mate yelled, "Get those hatches dogged down!" As I put the hatch clamps on, I kept one eye on the dock that was getting farther and farther away. Soon it disappeared into a cold, white fog. Thus began my first trip on a steamboat, the first of many trips that would fill a career for more than 30 years. The date was April 27, 1964.

We cleared the piers and, as I later learned, set a course for Copper Harbor. The ship's whistle sounded fog signals—three blasts every minute. After the deck was battened down, the mate let us off for the day. Most of the crew headed for the showers and to their rooms. Not me. I didn't feel like going to my quarters. I wanted to look this old girl over, so I started up the stairway toward the pilothouse. I walked around and finally the mate noticed me. "Would you like to see the inside of the wheelhouse?" he asked.

"Yes, sir!" was my response.

I met the wheelsman, Bill Liberty. "This guy must really know his stuff to steer such a big ship," I thought.

"How long have you been sailing?" I asked.

"About 25 years," he replied.

"Have you been in many storms?"

"Oh, just a few," he answered.

When the door opened and the first mate walked in, I thought, "This man must really know his stuff to be a first mate; he must be right next to God!"

The door opened again, and it was Captain Peter Peterson who came in. I thought, "Here is God!"

Captain Peterson was a kind, gentle old man, and we talked for a few minutes. Then the mate said, "You better go down and get some rest; morning comes early."

In my room, the only bunk that was empty was a top bunk, so I unpacked my clothes, showered, and jumped up into my new bed. It was too small. My feet touched the wire mesh at the end, but for tonight it would be fine. Two more deckhands arrived in the room, and I started asking Jim questions about my job. Jim had sailed for years, so he was my main man for information. One by one, we all fell asleep. It was the end of the first day.

Waking Up Early

Early the next morning, our door opened, all the lights came on, and we heard the deckwatch yell, "Everybody out of that sack!" It was his job to wake us up every morning. He really loved his job. Someday I would pay him back.

We sat down at the mess table to order our breakfast, and Ernie was his cheery self. Food gone, it was time to jump into our rain gear and boots and head for the deck and the hoses. We started at the forward cabins, hosing down all of the iron ore dust and then down on the main (spar) deck,

Iron ore pellets

hosing the stray pellets over the side. I thought there must be a furrow of iron ore pellets from Duluth all the way across Lake Superior from all the ships hosing down their decks while on the same course year after year.

At the end of our workday, we had finished hosing the deck and all the cabins. We made another visit to cheery Ernie for dinner, and then off for a hot shower. Next stop, the Soo Locks.

That night, I asked Jim to clue me in on what I must do on arrival at the Soo. "Don't worry about it," he said. "The mate will tell you what to do."

His answer wasn't good enough for me. I wanted details. I kept asking, and finally he gave me a rundown of what to expect. Then I was satisfied, but as I drifted off to sleep, I worried, "Will I be able to do my job?"

Out on deck the next morning, there was still a very thick fog. "Put on your life jackets and stand by," the mate ordered. (By then I knew what "stand by" meant.) I stood at the rail along the side of the ship trying to see through the fog, when all of a sudden, a wall came into view. We were at the Soo! "Wow!" I thought, "How did they find their way from Silver Bay to the Soo in this fog?" I thought that was the greatest feat in the world.

I was jolted from my thoughts by the mate's roar, "Dick, get over here and hop on this bosun's chair!" I did, and before I knew what was happening, I was flung over the side of a moving ship and hanging on to the chair's line for dear life. Bang! My feet hit the concrete on a dead run, and someone threw a heaving line from the deck right at me and into my face. I knew what to do now. I was at the Soo.

We entered the MacArthur Lock and tied the *Wilson* up with her wires. Wires taut and lock gates closed, the water level in the lock was lowered and in a few minutes we were at the level of Lake Huron. When the ship's gunwale (top edge) was even with the lock's edge, we all climbed back aboard. After one blast of the whistle (I didn't even jump this time, because I had been listening to the whistle's fog signals for 24 hours), the winches started heaving in the wires, and slowly "Big Tom" started moving ahead. We were underway once again. All my worry about what to do at the Soo was over. I did a good job. I considered myself a pro now.

Heading Down the St. Marys

As we headed downbound in the St. Marys River for the open waters of Lake Huron, the mate yelled, "Start soogie-ing the white work on the forward cabins!" ("Soogie-ing" means scrubbing the ship down.)

Soogie, soogie and soogie. That's all we ever did, every trip. I scrubbed the overhead with a brush on a long handle. The soogie ran down the handle and right up my sleeves into my armpits. I was wet all the time. Is this what it means to be a sailor, washing white work all of the time?

Later, I noticed the deckwatch didn't do much soogie-ing. He was always busy doing something else. "Hmm," I thought, "I could do his job." My sights were on a deckwatch job. To heck with this soogie-ing all of the time.

After an uneventful trip down Lake Huron and through the St. Clair and Detroit rivers, we arrived in Cleveland. When the ship was tied up, it was the deckhands' job to take the hatch clamps off. What a wail rose from the other deckhands! "Who

Thomas Wilson arriving in Cleveland; photo by Dick Metz

in the world (not exactly in those words) tightened all of these clamps so tight?" They looked at me.

Sheepishly, I admitted it was me, which was no surprise to them. I thought, "Darn you, Vince, again!"

The mate let off and said to be back aboard at midnight, so we all strolled uptown. It felt good to be on land where it was warm and there were no fog signals blowing. I felt I had been at sea for years instead of only two and a half days.

The *Wilson* underway; photo by Rudy Maki

MOVING UP

○-○○-○○-○○-○○-○○-○○-○○-○○

Ship: *Thomas Wilson*
Rank: Deckhand
Year: 1964

○-○○-○○-○○-○○-○○-○○-○○-○○

About midseason, the job was going along great. I knew all about being a deckhand, but I really wanted a deckwatch job. Deckwatches were on the job for four hours, followed by eight hours off, and then another four hours on. Deckhands were on watch for eight hours straight. Deckwatch was for me.

My chance came one day. Our deckwatch, Darrel—the guy who got his kicks every morning by waking us up so abruptly—was worried. "I don't know what to do," he said to me. "My girlfriend is pregnant. She keeps crying about how she wants me home by her. What should I do?"

I gave the situation some thought. Finally, I said, "Well, if I was in your predicament, I would decide to go home and marry the girl and be with her instead of out here on the lakes. You know, your wife and soon-to-be baby should come first."

Darrel thought about this for a few more days. When we arrived back at Duluth, he told the mate he was quitting to go home to take care of his new family. I shook his hand. "Goodbye, and best of luck to you." He left the ship, and I found myself the new deckwatch. For most of the rest of that season, I stayed deckwatch.

Working with Pappy

○○○○○○○○○○○○○○○○○
Ship: *Thomas Wilson*
Rank: Deckwatch
Year: 1964
○○○○○○○○○○○○○○○○○

Pappy was the watchman—my boss—on my watch, and we got along great together. From Mellen, Wisconsin, Pappy was a powerful man with huge arms and wrists so big he could not buy a watchband large enough to go around them. All the deckhands tried to beat Pappy at arm wrestling. He just laughed and smiled while puffing on his cigarette. With very little effort, he would bang their arms on the table. No one ever put him down.

One trip, after departing the MacArthur Lock downbound, we ran into fog, so the Old Man checked her speed down. He felt his way down the river as far as Lime Island.

When we were just below Lime Island, the visibility went right down to zero, and he decided to anchor. After he maneuvered into position, he yelled, "Let her go!" The anchor hit the water with a big splash, and the anchor chain came rumbling out, as it always did, sounding as if the ship was tearing herself apart. Everyone asleep up forward jumped a foot out of bed.

Getting Comfortable as Deckwatch

We lay at anchor until the next morning when the fog cleared. The Old Man told me to "raise the hook" (anchor) so we could get underway. As the windlass (anchor winch) pulled in the chain, we had a hose over the side to wash off the mud. When the anchor was just coming up through the water, we saw an old schooner anchor clinging to ours. It had a beautiful wooden stock with some old chain still attached. I called the Old Man in the pilothouse to tell him what we found. "We can tie some lines around it and lift it aboard," I suggested.

"Drop the anchor again and get rid of it; we don't have time to fool around with things like that." So we let our anchor go again, and when we hauled it back up, the old anchor was gone.

I soon became comfortable being a deckwatch. I was the one calling the watch and waking everyone each morning, but I wasn't like Darrel. I was like a mother to the guys. I would walk in and turn on a soft light and shake a guy's shoulder and say, "Time to get up."

Becoming an Able Seaman

○○○○○○○○○○○○○○○○○○

Ship: *Thomas Wilson*
Rank: Able Seaman
Year: 1965

○○○○○○○○○○○○○○○○○○

Now I was eyeing up the watchman's job! He was making more money than I was, and he was the deck boss. Most of the time, he stood watch on the bow, and he relieved the wheelsman for his coffee break. Then it was time for his own coffee break, and his watch was over. But before I could get a watchman's job, I would have to become an able seaman, or an "AB."

As soon as I got a chance, I went to the Coast Guard office in Duluth to ask for an able seaman manual and find out what the test would entail. "All the information is in the book," I was told. "All you have to do is study very hard."

Richard's Metz's Able Seaman ID card

Well, I did just what the Coast Guardsman said. Every night in my bunk, I studied and studied. During the day, I studied all the lifeboat equipment and what each piece was used for. I climbed the masts just to study the lights. I studied everything on that ship!

To obtain a lifeboat ticket (certificate), I had to lower a lifeboat into the water and take charge of the boat. We had a midsummer Coast Guard inspection that year, and when it came time to lower the boat into the water, the mate said that I was to take charge of the boat. "Do a good job, because the Coast Guard will be watching how the boat is handled. This will be your test."

We lowered the lifeboat, and the crew who were assigned to that boat climbed in and took their places. I ordered, "Up oars."

Pappy said to the crew, "I want all of you guys to listen to Dick's orders and do your best!" Everyone sat up straight and oars were all straight up.

I ordered, "Oars down, push away." All oars pushed away; each man had done his job. We rowed around for a while and then headed back to the ship. The mate and the Coast Guard were very pleased. Pappy had a lot to do with that.

Taking the Able Seaman Exam

The day finally arrived for me to write (take) my AB exam. I took a taxi from the dock to the Duluth Coast Guard building. I had no sooner taken out my AB manual and begun to page through it when the cab driver said, "We're here."

As I walked up to the steps leading to the main door, I wondered if I was ready. I wanted to pull out the manual and read it all over again. Then I thought, "If I don't know it now, I never will." I slipped the manual into my pocket and walked into the office. I filled out some paperwork, and the officer handed me the test.

I sat down. My mouth went dry. I was nervous. I got up enough courage to look at the first question. "I know that one," I said to myself, and wrote down the answer. I finished the test and felt pretty good about it as I handed it to the officer. Then I waited.

After a short while, he called me into his office. "Sit down," he said. He looked me right in the eye. "How did you study for this test?"

My heart sank. The palms of my hands started to sweat. "How could I have flunked this test?" I thought. I had felt so good about it. I was numb. My AB career was down the drain. That did it. I'd have to go back home because I could not face the crew after all they did for me and I failed the test.

"Mr. Metz?"

I was jolted from my stupor. "Oh! Yes, sir! I studied my manual day and night and learned by looking at all the ship's equipment from the anchor to the stern light, and the crew all pitched in to help me, sir."

He was silent for a few seconds. Again he looked me in the eye and said, "Well, Mr. Metz (oh, no, here it comes), you have the highest score on your test that has ever been recorded in this office."

I couldn't believe what he said! What a change in the wind. He continued, "Any man who can write a perfect score like this should consider writing for a mate's license as soon as he has enough sea time." He stood up; I stood up. He shook my hand, congratulated me, and God carried me through his door.

I felt great. I was proud of myself because all of my studying had paid off. I walked over to the clerk, a charming young lady with a smile on her face. As she handed me my brand new AB card, she said, "I hear you did very well on your test."

"Yes, I did. How would you like to go out for dinner and celebrate with me?" She accepted my invitation.

When I walked back aboard the *Thomas Wilson*, Captain Peterson was standing next to the boarding ladder. He asked, "Are you an AB?"

"Yes, sir!" I answered with my head held high.

"Good, you're on the 12 to 4 watch as watchman. Bill Anderson retired today while you were gone." Bill, a fine shipmate and friend, lived in Duluth and had been sailing for 30 years. Life was great. Here I was, a new AB, and a watchman with a raise in pay. Little did I know then, I would not be satisfied for long with my new job.

Downsides of the Job

Being a watchman required me to stand lookout on the bow in all kinds of weather. One morning on Lake Superior, I was on bow lookout with a Nor'easter blowing a gale. We were heading right into it. Seas were coming over the bow as the ship nosedived into each oncoming wave. My oilskins (cold-weather gear) were covered with ice. The mate was crazy for having me standing out here in weather like this! Oh, well, I wanted to be a watchman, so here I was.

It started snowing, and the mate started blowing fog signals. He lowered the front pilothouse window and yelled down to me, "Do you hear another ship's fog signal, and if you do, where is it? I have a ship on radar!"

Here I was, standing on the bow with seas pouring over me, a howling wind blowing into my face, taking my breath away, our fog signal blowing three blasts every minute yet I could barely make out the sound 600 feet away, and thick snow swirling into my eyes.

How in the world did he expect me to hear or see another ship? I have never forgotten that hellish night, especially after I became mate.

A (Very) Close Call

Another time we were upbound hauling around Southeast Shoal in Lake Erie in dense fog, and I was standing bow on lookout for over three hours. The wind was light, it was a quiet day, and the only sound was that of the bow pushing the water aside as we moved through it. Just before my watch ended, my relief walked up and we talked for a few minutes about the weather and the fog.

"Have you heard any other ships around?" he asked.

"No, we're all alone out here. No other ships around. Have a good watch." I walked off the bow.

Just before I got to my room, I heard five short blasts from our whistle: the danger signal. I was confused about why the danger signal was blowing, so I ran back up on deck. Looking over to port, I saw a huge ship's bow appear out of the fog heading straight for us. The name *Charles C. West* was painted in big, black letters across the front of the pilothouse. Where did she come from? I hadn't heard the *West* blowing fog signals.

Her port bow came up on our port side. She was turning to avoid hitting our ship, and she did it just in time!

Her bow scraped all the way aft along our ship's side. Sparks flew. I smelled paint burning as she slid along. When her stern met our stern, our port lifeboat was smashed.

Then the *West* disappeared into the fog just as silently as she had come. I ran up to the pilothouse to ask the mate what had happened. He didn't say a word, but I saw his ashen face. The Captain was still standing in the front window with his right hand fumbling for the general alarm.

Steering the Ship

Ship: *Thomas Wilson*
Rank: Able Seaman, Watchman
Year: 1965

Part of my duties included relieving the wheelsman for his 20-minute coffee break once during each watch. This was right up my alley, as it meant I headed up into the "brain box" where navigating the ship took place. I loved being behind the wheel and steering this monster of a ship, making her head for each course that the mate barked out. At first, it was just out in the waters of the open lake.

After I got good at steering in mid-lake, I got to relieve on the wheel in the rivers. What a job! I enjoyed standing at the helm and looking out of the pilothouse windows, watching the shoreline pass by. It was so good to see small craft with girls wearing bikinis waving to us and meeting passing ships. But most of all, it was warm in the winter and cool in the summer and there was no standing out on the bow. This was the job for me!

A sign of things to come; photo by Dick Metz

Becoming a Wheelsman

○○○○○○○○○○○○○○○○○

Ship: *Thomas Wilson*
Rank: Wheelsman
Year: 1965

○○○○○○○○○○○○○○○○○

We had a wheelsman from Virginia named Willie. A laid-back individual with a great sense of humor, for him life was fun and much of it was a joke. One day, we were downbound in the St. Clair River just about parallel to Fawn Island, a flat, pretty little island with green grass and a few homes, that sits low in the water. When we got to the buoy, the captain ordered a course change to port.

He noticed the ship was not turning, and immediately said, "Port," again.

Still the ship did not respond.

Once more, "*Port!*" he shouted.

Ol' Willie said, "I can't, Cap. The wheel fell off." Willie stood there with the wheel in his hand, not one bit excited. The ship by now was headed straight for Fawn Island.

The captain about bit his pipe in half. The mate ran from the chart room into the pilothouse, grabbed the wheel from Willie, replaced it on its shaft, and got control of the ship.

"You take the wheel," the captain said to me. He turned to Willie. "You're fired!"

I had my wheelsman's job. I remembered back to when I worked at the paper mill. Yes, now I considered myself the luckiest person in the world.

Lay Up and a Practical Joke

We laid up (idled the ship during the winter) that year in Ashtabula, Ohio. After we had completed all the end-of-the-season tasks that readied the *Wilson* to sit safely moored while the lakes iced over, we were ready to leave the ship and head for home.

"You can't go home yet," the mate told us. He said we had to wait for the fleet's flagship, the steamer *Joseph S. Wood*, to arrive and then help lay her up. We weren't very happy about that.

"Let's go up to the sailors' bar for a drink," suggested Pappy.

We all agreed, though none of us had ever been in that bar before. It was within walking distance, and as we walked, we questioned Pappy about what kind of bar he was taking us to. He grinned and said, "You'll see."

Richard Metz's Merchant Mariner's Certificate

"It must be something really special," I thought.

We entered the building like a flock of sheep. We crossed the first room to a heavy, oak door with a little slit in the center. On the other side of the door, the slit opened and all we saw was an eyeball peering through at us. "Show me your AB cards," we heard.

"Man, this is really something with all this security," I thought. I really didn't know what to expect behind that oak door. I slipped my AB card through the slit, the eyeball looked at it, and a buzzer sounded. The big door opened and we walked in. Everything seemed normal; the bar was at the far end of the room. But the room was empty! No one was sitting at the bar or any other place in that room. As I sat down at the bar and ordered a drink, my eyes traveled all around that empty room. I waited for something to happen. Nothing did.

We had a few drinks and decided to head back to the ship. Pappy stayed behind at the bar with a grin still on his face. What a guy. He had gotten our hopes up and then found nothing but a dead place. Of course, he never promised us anything. It didn't matter; we would get even with him.

The *Wood* finally arrived at Ashtabula the next day. Our deckhands and wheelsmen walked over to the *Wood* and worked the rest of the day to lay her up for the winter. Now we could go home.

Getting Payback

After breakfast the next morning, we went back to our rooms to pack our bags. Pappy's seabag, packed and ready to go, was already sitting on the deck outside his door. "Now is the time to get even," I said. "Go on deck and bring back some iron ore."

Meanwhile, I opened up his bag, and removed some of his gear. The others came back with about ten pounds of iron ore that they were able to shovel up from what had been spilled on deck. I dumped it into the bottom of Pappy's bag and repacked his gear.

"Your cab is here," the mate called.

We all picked up our seabags, slung them over our shoulders, and watched Pappy do the same. It was a long walk out and through the dock gate to the waiting taxi. "Man, I didn't think I had that much gear in my bag," said Pappy, puffing as he lifted it into the cab's trunk. We all turned our heads so he couldn't see our smiling faces or hear our stifled laughter.

All of us got on a bus that was heading toward Chicago. One by one, each man got off at his station except for Pappy and me. We traveled together beyond Chicago, as both of us lived in Wisconsin.

In a little farm town in central Wisconsin, the bus stopped for a lunch break. "We'll stop for 45 minutes. Everybody be aboard then so we can stay on schedule," the driver announced. Everyone else went into the small cafe where we had stopped. But not Pappy and me.

We looked up Main Street and headed toward a hotel on the corner. We heard a polka band playing. We looked inside the door. "Come on in," someone said. So we did.

It was a Polish wedding. Everyone was happy and having a good time dancing. After a few drinks, Pappy and I just fit right in and had a ball! I was dancing with the bride when the bus driver burst into the room. "You, there, get back on the bus! I've looked all over this town for you. Now we're behind schedule," he snarled.

"Why don't you stay?" asked the groom. "In a few days you can get a ride home."

"No, but thanks anyway," I said. "Thanks for a good time."

We got back on the bus. We were not very popular with the driver or the passengers for the rest of the trip. With every bus change, Pappy had picked up his bag and threw it over his shoulder, grunting. He never did figure out why it was so heavy.

The *Thomas Wilson* passes the *Joseph Wood;* photo by Dick Metz

STEERING BY THE STARS

○○○○○○○○○○○○○○○○○○

Ship: *Thomas Wilson*
Rank: Deckhand
Year: 1964

○○○○○○○○○○○○○○○○○○

In 1964, I was a deckhand aboard the *Thomas Wilson*. Early one morning, we got word that we had to go on deck because of an emergency. We all got up, dressed and out on deck we went. I noticed the ship was dead in the water and the out of command lights were on (they informed other ships that we couldn't control the *Wilson*).

We all wondered what was wrong. It was not long before we found out. The mate came down from the wheelhouse yelling that everybody had to get to the back of the boat. The night was clear and calm, and we were just off Devils Island Light in Lake

Superior. We got back aft, and the chief engineer told us the steering gear had failed and that we could not steer the ship. We were ordered to the boat deck to use the emergency steering wheel. The chief had put the gear in and with a walkie-talkie said for us to try to move the big brass wheel. Two men on each side of the wheel tried to make it move, but it was frozen in place. It hadn't been used for years. Another upbound steamer had slowed down and was ready to take us in tow. However, the chief said to the Old Man that he had another idea, and he would like to try it. The captain agreed.

An Ingenious Fix

The *Wilson* was equipped with six steam-powered mooring winches. The chief had the bright idea to use the two back winches, one on each side, to steer the ship. We did so by running the wire cables from each winch around the stern of the ship and attaching one wire to the rudder from the port side and the other wire around the starboard side of the ship back to the rudder. The chief put a small punt (a small boat) into the water, and we hauled the wires around back to the fantail, the very back of the ship. We lowered the eye of the port wire down to the men in the boat; they attached the eye of the wire to the rudder by using a clevis, a metal fastener. When that wire was secured to the rudder, we handed him the starboard wire and the same procedure was performed. Job finished, the chief reported to the captain that we were ready to get underway. The old steam engine belched out a plume of black smoke, and we started ahead very slowly.

Steering Like a Wounded Duck

The idea was to have the captain up on the bridge give a compass heading for Duluth. The mate sat between the two winches and operated the steam valves from each winch, using the winches on each side to steer the ship. The captain would say over the walkie-talkie to come to port so many degrees, then starboard so many degrees. The plan was not working out very well. The ship was going up the lake from side to side like a wounded duck. I sat with the walkie-talkie, giving the mate courses to steer, and I came up with an idea. I said to the mate I would take over and he could rest a bit. My first idea was to keep the ship from going from side by side by keeping both steam valves cracked open just a touch. When the captain yelled a new heading, I would close one valve to cut the steam off on one winch and keep the other valve cracked open. By doing this, she started to steer on the heading given. It was a clear night with all the stars shining.

The Wilson underway; photo by Dick Metz

Steering by a Star

I noticed one star was in line with the forward mast when we were on course. "I'll steer on that star," I thought to myself. I sat between the two winches, steering with the mast on one star and then another star to keep the ship on course. The mate said he would put me on overtime if I stayed on the winches, and he said

I was doing pretty well. Most of all, this plan gave the tired captain time to relax. Early the next morning, two Great Lakes tugs came out to tow us in to the shipyard. I was tired by then, and the mate gave me the day off, with pay.

I started to wonder how long it had been since a ship was steered by the stars on the lakes. I was a hero to my shipmates, at least for a day.

The *Woodrush*; U.S. Coast Guard photo

I'LL NEVER FORGET
THE *WOODRUSH*

∘⚬∘⚬∘⚬∘⚬∘⚬∘⚬∘⚬∘

Ship: *Thomas Wilson*
Rank: Able Seaman, Watchman
Year: 1964

∘⚬∘⚬∘⚬∘⚬∘⚬∘⚬∘⚬∘

Author's note: *This story tells of an unfortunate incident that we hope will never again be repeated. The bad has to be told with the good. A lot of people out there will probably not want to hear this story about the Coast Guard or the Coast Guard Cutter Woodrush.*

We met her off Eagle Harbor at 0130 on November 29, 1964.

In 1964, I was an able seaman watchman on the *Thomas Wilson*. Late one night while upbound on Lake Superior, I walked up to the wheelhouse to relieve the wheelsman for a coffee break.

39

The mate on watch had a target on radar. It showed the target was headed downbound (toward the Atlantic), but on the upbound course, and closing fast.

The mate radioed the vessel, and the *Woodrush* answered saying they had our vessel on radar and not to worry and hold our course and speed, which the mate did. When the wheelsman finished his coffee break, he took over the wheel and again the mate called the *Woodrush* saying they were on a collision course. The *Woodrush* replied by saying that they saw us and again not to worry.

I figured, well, they must know what they are doing, being the Coast Guard, and I walked back to the galley for my coffee. While in the galley the ship took a sharp roll to starboard. I got up to look out of a porthole and all I saw was a black shape just missing our ship by a matter of feet. Back up in the wheelhouse the captain was up and saying the *Woodrush* never altered her course and if we had not altered ours, a collision would have occurred.

That next winter I stopped in a cafe for coffee at Bruce Crossing, Michigan. I noticed a sailor sitting there, so I started talking to him. He said he had missed the bus for Duluth. I offered to drive him to Duluth and while underway I told him I sailed on the lakes and he said he was assigned to the *Woodrush*. I told him the story about the near collision and I was shocked to learn that he was aboard the cutter that night and was the helmsmen when this all took place. I asked him what had happened, why did they not alter course. The young man said they were all drinking that night and were all messed up.

I will never forget the *Woodrush*!

The *B.F. Jones*; photo by Dick Metz

WRONG SIDE OF THE BUOY

○-○-○-○-○-○-○-○-○-○-○-○-○-○-○-○

Ship: *B. F. Jones*
Rank: Able Seaman, Wheelsman
Year: 1966

○-○-○-○-○-○-○-○-○-○-○-○-○-○-○-○

As the weather shows signs of warming after the deep of winter, sailors await orders from their company. They are told to report aboard a certain ship at a specific time and date. Sometimes they're happy with their assignments, but sometimes they aren't.

In spring of 1966, the company sent me orders to report aboard the steamer *B. F. Jones* as wheelsman.

I didn't like the *Jones*. She was small. She was built in 1904 and had cramped living quarters. She had 18 telescoping hatches—hatches with metal sections that overlapped—and each needed a tarp placed over it to prevent water from seeping in.

41

I wanted the "Big Tom" back. I knew her from stem to stern and everybody who sailed on her. I had cut my teeth on that ship, so to speak. She was comfortable; she was home.

But, like it or not, I found myself on the *Jones*. Four men slept in a small cabin with only one porthole. When a man wanted to leave the room, the other three had to jump into their bunks in order to let him out.

The pilothouse was extremely small, too. With the wheelsman standing on "monkey island" (his raised platform one step above the pilothouse's deck), the captain and the mate on watch had to make room for each other to walk around. The ship was fitted with a large brass helm, but it was hand steering only; there was no automatic pilot like the "Big Tom" had. After four hours on the brass helm, my hands were dirty and smelled of brass. I didn't like the *Jones* at all.

After a few months on the *B. F. Jones*, I just could not make myself like this ship. I asked to be transferred to either the *Wilson* or the *Wood*, but there were no wheeling jobs available on either ship.

One morning as we departed the MacArthur Lock after locking down (heading away from Lake Superior), fog set in. It was thick as we rounded Mission Point. The mate said to the captain, "There's an upbound ship coming our way, and she's Canadian." In those days, Americans didn't think Canadian sailors were very good navigators and thought they were drunk most of the time. Our captain did not like meeting their ships in the fog at close quarters.

The mate kept his eyes on the radar and watched the ship get closer and closer.

The captain shouted a course for me to steer, and he wanted no deviation. "Nothing to port and nothing to starboard!"

I said to myself, "He must think we are on railroad tracks instead of a river with a current pushing us along." I watched that gyrocompass like a hawk to keep on my course. On a gyrocompass, when the ship moves a quarter degree to either side of the current heading, there's a click. Well, she started clicking, and my hands started to sweat. I hoped the Old Man would not hear the click. He didn't, because he was making clicking noises himself.

The NOAA Chart for Mission Point

The two ships passed side by side in the thick fog. All we saw was a white glow from the deck lights on that Canadian ship.

Years later, when I sailed on Canadian ships, I learned that their crews were not drunks, and that they are, in fact, some of the finest ship handlers in the world.

Back on the Wilson

Ship: *Thomas Wilson*
Rank: Able Seaman, Wheelsman
Year: 1966

In November 1966, I was wheeling aboard the steamer *Thomas Wilson* on the 12 to 4 watch. The third mate was studying

43

for his first class pilot's license while on watch and not paying too much attention to the ship's position. After a while, he got up from his chair and started looking off to the port side through his binoculars.

He looked for a bit, and I said, "What are you looking for?"

"A green lighted buoy."

I looked, too, but couldn't see it. Then I looked over to the starboard side. "There's a flashing green off to starboard," I reported.

He turned to look. "Hard to starboard!" he yelled.

I jumped behind the wheel, switched to hand steering from the iron mike, and flung the wheel hard over to the starboard. We had missed the reef by feet.

The ship was empty, except for ballast, so when she started to turn, she had listed over to port. This, of course, caused the captain to ring up the bridge. "What's going on?"

A green navigation buoy

The mate responded sheepishly, "We were on the wrong side of the green buoy, but she's back on course now."

The captain came up to the pilothouse. "You wanted to be a first class pilot? Well, you wouldn't make a first class dishwasher!" He made a few other choice comments.

Then he said, "You're fired!"

When we came to the same position on our next trip upbound, I was on watch with a different third mate. It was a beautiful sunny day with calm seas. We saw that green buoy from far away. And alongside that buoy was the grounded oceangoing ship Nordmeer, the remnants of which now rest on top of the reef.

Dreaming of Isle Royale

Ship: *Thomas Wilson*
Rank: Able Seaman, Wheelsman
Year: 1966

While on western Lake Superior headed for Duluth one morning, I noticed a vessel crossing ahead of us. I picked up the binoculars to take a closer look. It was the ferry *Ranger III* out of Houghton, Michigan, carrying a load of passengers to Isle Royale National Park.

Isle Royale is situated about 70 miles of Michigan's Keweenaw Peninsula and is about 50 miles long by 12 miles wide. Popular with hikers and campers, Isle Royale National Park also has two beautiful lodges, one at Windigo on the southwestern end of the island, and one at Rock Harbor on the northeastern end.

Ranger III and her passengers were headed for Rock Harbor. The *Ranger* was a nice-looking ship, about 165 feet long, painted light blue and cream and moving at about 12 knots.

I realized it had been several years since I had been to Isle Royale, where I spent time diving on the shipwrecks that dot the island's coast. I wanted to go back to the island again, but how?

A few days passed, but I couldn't get Isle Royale out of my mind. I really wanted to go back. Then the answer came to me: Simple, send a resume.

The *J.E. Colombe*; taken by Dick Metz

ME? A TUGBOAT CAPTAIN?

ooooooooooooooooo

Ship: *J. E. Colombe*
Rank: Tugboat Captain
Year: 1966

ooooooooooooooooo

As soon as we got back to Buffalo with a load of grain, I sent the National Park Service my resume and asked whether they had an opening for an able seaman on the *Ranger III*. I figured all I could do was wait; I assumed I didn't have much of a chance of getting a job on the *Ranger*.

A week later, my friend Vince placed a shore-to-ship call. "Dick," he said, "there was a call from the National Park Service. They asked for you. They want you to call their office in Houghton."

I phoned the National Park Service office ship-to-shore immediately after hanging up from Vince. "We've got an able seaman job open. Do you want it?" they asked.

Of course, I wanted it! "I'll take it," I said. "When do I need to be there?"

"Tomorrow." My spirits sank.

"Well, I'm two days from Duluth," I said, "and I have to give the Old Man some notice."

"Okay," was the reply. "Call our office as soon as you leave your ship in Duluth."

We docked in Duluth, and I was gone. I headed for the nearest phone and called the NPS. "I'm off the ship and ready to fly to Houghton," I told the girl on the other end of the line.

"I'm sorry, the job has been filled."

I couldn't speak; I was so shocked! That was the worst news I could hear. After I composed myself, I said, "Lady, I just quit my job for the able seaman job that you said was mine."

"Sorry, we had to fill it," she said. "But we do need a captain for our tugboat. Would you be interested in that position?"

"Well," I hesitated. "I don't know anything about tugboats. I've never been aboard one. But I do need a job…"

"You will be trained," she assured me.

What else could I do but say, "Yes."

"Okay, great." Then she added, "But first you have to go to the Coast Guard and write for a small boat license."

"Well, all right." It seemed to me that I had no choice now.

A few days later, I arrived at the NPS office in Houghton with license in hand, half expecting the tug job to be gone, too. But I was in luck this time. I was hired.

Morning came, and I found myself tightly strapped into a Cessna floatplane flying across Lake Superior. I was headed for my new life and position on Isle Royale. It was exciting when the island came into view. It looked beautiful from the air with green pine trees covering the rocks everywhere. There were small bays and inlets with clear blue water, so clear I could make out the rocks and reefs forty feet down. It was majestic, truly God's creation, and I remember thinking that He threw His watch away after creating this paradise. This was to be my island.

The *J. E. Colombe*

The pilot brought the plane down in the area of Rock Harbor. While we taxied to the dock, I looked out the window and saw the tug *J. E. Colombe* tied up and waiting for her new skipper.

The pilot pointed to a park ranger standing on the dock in his green and gray uniform with a Smoky Bear hat, "There's the man you have to see."

I climbed out of the plane and walked up the dock. I set my bags on the ground and introduced myself.

"Follow me to your quarters," the ranger instructed. I shouldered my bags again and followed him up a trail to a dormitory where I threw my gear on the bed. I turned around and went back to have a look at the tug.

It seemed like a nice tug, 45 feet long with a 170-horsepower Buda diesel engine. The engine room was clean, as were the crew quarters. The pilothouse was equipped with an AM marine radio and a magnetic compass, but no radar.

Frank, the mechanic, came aboard and showed me how to start the generator and main engine.

"Do you know when my trainer is going to get here to show me how to operate this thing?" I asked.

"There is no trainer coming," Frank replied.

"Oh, boy," I thought, "I should have stayed wheeling on the big boats."

Mott Island and the Algoma

Mott Island is the National Park Service headquarters for Isle Royale National Park. It's a very small island, only one mile long and half a mile wide. It's basically a huge rock covered with pine trees, and this was now my home and the center of my career. Little did I know then that I'd spend the next seven years there.

Wanting to explore my new home, I spotted a path leading off into the island's interior and followed it into a deep pine forest. The sweet aroma of the pines combined with the heat of the earth. Eventually the path led to the Superior shoreline, dotted with numerous rocky bays and inlets, where I found myself atop a rocky cliff. Far below was a deep pool of clear water. Looking down, I could see the remains of a ship below the surface of the calm water.

The wreck was the Canadian passenger steamer *Algoma*, which had broken in two during a storm in 1885. Forty-six people lost their lives right here.

After a hearty breakfast at the mess hall the next morning, I walked down the hill to the *Colombe*. In came the seaplane, and out stepped my deckhand, Joe.

"How long you been tugging?" he asked as we shook hands.

I looked at my watch. "Just about one day now."

"Well, you've been doin' it longer than me," he said. "You've gotta train me, 'cause I've never been on a tugboat."

So we trained ourselves over the next few days. We practiced with the tug running up and down the harbor, going full ahead and full astern. Soon we were ready for the barges. We took the tug into the barge cove where they were all tied up, and secured the tug alongside a barge with a large deck-mounted crane. This barge was 85 feet long and 35 feet wide, and in addition to the crane, contained crew quarters, a welding shop, and a bin for loading rock.

Present-day Rock Harbor on Isle Royale

John Murn, the superintendent of construction, greeted us and gave us a tour. "You need to tow the barge to the north end of the island, so I can load rock from the bottom of the harbor." We didn't do so well on this first tow, but after a few more weeks passed, we learned how.

In addition to the rock barges, our mission was to haul all the supplies that the park needed for its seasonal operations. This included gasoline, diesel fuel and building materials, which we barged from Houghton, Michigan, back to Isle Royale, a distance of 70 miles.

One afternoon, we received orders to prepare the *Colombe* and three gas barges to leave the next morning for Houghton where we would load 35,000 gallons of gasoline.

Joe and I lined up all the barges in a row with towlines attached and waited for morning. I was on the tug at 0400, getting the latest marine weather forecast over the old AM radio. It looked good, so Joe and I departed the dock with the line of barges stretching 1,000 feet behind us.

We had to navigate Middle Island Passage to get out on the big lake. The passage was very narrow, with three buoys marking the deep-water channel. The only navigational aid at the entrance to the passage was an old foghorn. It sounded like a dying moose. We wormed our way through that passage out to the lake, and our trip over to Houghton was uneventful.

Houghton, Michigan, today

In Houghton, we filled the barges with gasoline and headed back to the island.

Before we knew it, thick fog set in. We gave security calls over the radio every 15 minutes advising our position. The route back to the island involved crossing one of the world's busiest shipping lanes—traffic in and out of Duluth-Superior. And we were crossing at the speed of a whopping five miles per hour. In fact, we crossed right in front of two ships heading for Duluth. Both ships answered our security calls and told us that their radars could not pick up the three barges full of gasoline that we were towing behind the *Colombe*.

One captain was a bit upset about this and informed me that this was not the place for me to be without radar on my tug. He was right!

I hoped the fog would clear before we arrived at the passage, but no such luck. We'd been on the water for 14 hours, so I figured we had to be getting close to the island, although we could not see anything.

I radioed the office on Isle Royale and said, "Have the fog-horn turned on." I thought that hearing the horn would give me some idea how far out from the island we were. Well, the horn was on, but we didn't hear it. I didn't want to chance going in closer and possibly running up on the rocks. So we turned and headed back out, ran for 30 minutes, turned again for the passage and ran for 30 minutes. We kept this up until the fog lifted some. Then we finally heard the dying moose wail of the foghorn and headed toward it. We found the buoys and the deep-water channel.

After that experience, I explained to the Park Service the danger involved when crossing the lake in fog and trying to find our way back through the passage. I told them that that was it for me, no more crossings until we had radar installed on the tug. They agreed.

We did go back to Houghton once more without radar, but our new Decca radar was installed while we were loading building materials there. The equipment worked flawlessly. As we headed back across the lake, I thought, "Just let it fog up now." It stayed clear as a bell.

About ten miles out, we met the *Ranger III* headed for Houghton. Captain Woody called and informed us, "We've had a set to the west all the way over from the island." (This meant that the tug was drifting to the west because of an east wind.)

We changed course for the correction to more of a north-easterly heading. On our new radar, we saw the Michigan shoreline clearly, and several ships coming and going. It was a perfect day, and looked like it would be a perfect trip all the way back to the island.

Wrong. After about ten hours, the sky became darker. Black clouds formed, and the wind freshened from the southwest. The sea began lapping over the sides of the *Colombe*, and soon the tug was rolling from side to side. The sky became a mass of clouds, the waves grew, and it started to rain. I checked the barges through my field glasses. As waves boiled over the top of each barge, they were briefly under water. Night fell early. It wasn't fun, but at least we had our radar. Or did we?

"Something's wrong with this radar," Joe said.

I looked into the display, and the scanner was barely moving as it made its sweep. This was accompanied by a strange noise. "Take the wheel, Joe. I'm going to check the engine room," I said.

I quickly found the problem: the generator was failing. All electric power would soon be gone—lights, radio, and the radar. I turned off everything except the old AM radio transmitter to conserve what battery power I had left. "Tug *Colombe* to Park office," I radioed. Someone at the office monitored the radio at all times when we crossed the lake. No answer. "Tug *Colombe* calling the Park Service," I tried again and again. We could not raise a soul.

I could see a heavy squall approaching. The rain increased, as did the wind, and the sky was a web of lightning. "We're in one hell of a fix," I said as much to myself as to Joe. "No generator, no lights, no radar, and no communication with anyone. And we don't even know our exact position."

When the lightning flashed, I could make out Joe's worried expression. "What are we gonna do?" he asked. I could see in his expression that he hoped I had a solution.

Waves crash on Isle Royale

"At the moment, I really don't know."

The tug rolled hard, but she was seaworthy. I wondered how the barges were doing behind us, but I couldn't see them at all. "Oh, well, to heck worrying about the barges; what are we going to do about us?" I thought.

I said to Joe, "The only thing we've got left to navigate with is the old radio direction finder." The only thing I had ever used the small, battery-powered radio direction finder for was to play music. An antiquated piece of equipment, a radio direction finder does exactly what it says—it helps you find the direction of a radio source, enabling you to navigate. Most vessels used more modern technology; using RDF to navigate was the equivalent of using an electronic lighthouse.

Plus, I didn't even know if the direction finder part of it worked, but it was worth a try. I turned it on and tried to get an radio direction finder bearing from Passage Island Lighthouse, but I couldn't get anything from inside the pilothouse. I would have to go out on deck and try.

I pulled on rain gear and a life jacket, and stuffed the portable device under the rain jacket where it would stay dry.

It was not inviting outside. I opened the door of the pilothouse that was out of the wind, and I looked behind to make sure Joe was at the wheel.

"Be careful!" Joe had to shout to be heard above the noise of the storm.

It was impossible to stand up outside because of the wind, rain, waves, and the rolling and pitching of the tug. I got down on my belly and crawled up the deck to the bow with the device under my arm inside the rain jacket. The lightning was so intense and the thunder so loud that I smelled smoke with each crack. The lake was lit up for miles with each lightning bolt. I could see the mountainous waves. "What I would give to be back aboard a big ship and cozy in a warm, dry bunk," I thought.

As I reached the bow, Joe reduced the tug's speed to keep the bow from dipping into each approaching wave. I laid the RDF on deck and turned the dial to get a bearing from Passage Island. Water washed over the bow, the RDF got wet, and I was soaked to the skin. But then I heard it faintly: . . - - -

It was the Morse code from Passage Island. I took a bearing and motioned Joe to alter course. I stayed there and listened some more. The Morse code got louder. I had it!

I crawled and slid back to the pilothouse door. Safely back inside, I shed my rain gear and reached for a hot cup of coffee. We remained on that heading until we could hear the foghorn blowing off Passage Island Light. The lighthouse was situated four miles off the northeastern tip of Isle Royale. Now my only problem was finding the entrance to Rock Harbor.

We had come in close to the light off Passage Island and turned toward the island to try to pick out Blake's Point Light.

"Turn on the radar one more time and see what happens," Joe urged.

I fully expected to see nothing, but amazingly, I could see the tip of the island. I could just barely make out the harbor entrance, but that was all we needed. Finally, we were inside and back home.

The *John Dykstra*; photo by Dick Metz

ARE YOU TRYING TO KILL US?

Ship: *John Dykstra*
Rank: Able Seaman, Wheelsman
Year: 1968

In the fall of 1968, I was a wheelsman on the steamer *John Dykstra* for the Ford Motor Company. Our captain was an old saltwater sailor and was used to heavy seas.

When we departed the Soo Locks for Superior, Wisconsin, we were in ballast (empty except for the ballast tanks), which meant the ship would roll more if there was heavy weather. I noticed that the US Coast Guard was displaying two red pennants from their station: gale warnings were expected on Lake Superior.

As we steamed toward Whitefish Point, I saw many ships going to anchor behind the point to wait out the approaching

59

storm. I wondered what our captain was going to do. Would he decide to anchor like the other ships, or continue out into the gale?

Well, the captain sat in the front window and never said a word about the anchored ships, the gale warnings, or what his intention was. One by one, we steamed past the ships at anchor, and I soon guessed what we were going to do. I wanted to see what he had to say, so I threw a comment his way. "Cap," I said, "it looks like a little city over there with all the lights from the ships that are at anchor."

"Yes, lots of lights over there," was his reply. We rounded the point and set our course across the lake.

When we came to our course, which would take us across the middle of the big lake, I put the steering gear on automatic. The mate took over from the Old Man. The captain turned to me and said, "Richard, we are going to make Christians out of these sailors tonight."

I gulped, "Yes, sir."

I finished my watch that night, and before I climbed into my bunk, I secured everything in my room. I knew we would be in for a wild ride the next day.

In the Teeth of the Storm

When I awoke and went aft for lunch, the wind had whipped up a good sea from the northeast, and the ship was rolling. The cook had all the tablecloths wetted down so that the dishes would not slide off the table.

I went to the pilothouse for my watch and found the Old Man there on the bridge with the mate. I relieved the wheel, took the steering off automatic, and put it on hand steering. We were rolling so badly that the automatic pilot would not hold the course.

Soon we found ourselves right in the middle of a Nor'easter. I tried to keep the ship on course, but because of rolling from side to side, I had a hard time keeping her steady.

My legs were spread as far apart as they would go. I had to hang on to the wheel in order to stay at my station.

The Old Man kept yelling, "Keep her on course!"

"This is crazy," I thought. "We should be at anchor with the other ships behind the point."

I could not keep her on course. The seas were rolling right over the deck. I told the Old Man this. He never said a word.

The symbol for a gale warning

Finally, the third mate could stand it no longer. He yelled to the Old Man, "What's the matter with you? Are you nuts? Are you trying to kill all of us?"

I was stunned. No one ever talked to a captain like that. But I was happy that the mate had yelled at him. The captain came over to me, and in a very quiet, calm voice said, "Richard, put her head into the sea."

After we put her head into the wind and sea, the captain checked her speed down because when the propeller came out of the water the whole ship would shake.

The captain went down to his quarters, and the mate went about his duties.

Nothing else was ever said about the incident.

The T-Harbor, taken from atop the Sleeping Giant

ACROSS THE BORDER

Ship: *Georgian Bay*
Rank: Able Seaman, Wheelsman
Year: 1973

It was early October 1973 when I left Houghton. I decided to drive around Lake Superior and head up to Thunder Bay, Ontario, to visit my dad, who lived east of Thunder Bay.

From his house I could see the Sleeping Giant, the contour of the Sibley Peninsula that formed one side of the bay and looked like a reclining giant. Pie Island stood tall on the opposite side of the giant with Isle Royale in the center. I mentioned to Dad what a nice view he had.

I had stayed with Dad for a while every year. As he was a resident of Canada, he wanted me to get Landed Immigrant

Status, so he sponsored me with a commitment of five years, and I was admitted to Canada in 1973.

"Why don't you sail on a Canadian ship for the rest of this year?" Dad suggested. "They come into Thunder Bay."

I knew they were short of seamen, so I thought about it, and agreed. "I'll check in at the Seafarers International Union hall in the morning."

First, I went to the Canadian Coast Guard office and proudly displayed my US license, which they said was not valid in Canada for a mate's job. However, I could go out as a wheelsman. That was all right with me, so I went to the hall and signed up.

Joining the *Georgian Bay*

ᴑᴑᴑᴑᴑᴑᴑᴑᴑᴑᴑᴑᴑᴑᴑᴑ

Ship: *Georgian Bay*
Rank: Able Seaman, Wheelsman
Year: 1973

ᴑᴑᴑᴑᴑᴑᴑᴑᴑᴑᴑᴑᴑᴑᴑᴑ

There were two ships currently in the harbor looking for a wheelsman. One was *Silver Isle*; the other was *Georgian Bay*. I liked the name *Georgian Bay*, so I chose her.

When I got to the grain elevator, I found that the *Georgian Bay* was nearly loaded and would be departing shortly. The mate took me up to meet the captain. I realized that he would want to see my discharge book (the record of all the ships a sailor has sailed on, and the positions held), but I had forgotten it.

The captain was a gruff old man with many years of sailing experience. "Let me see your discharge book."

"I forgot it," I said sheepishly.

"Well, we're about to leave. I don't have time to call the hall for another wheelsman, so I will take your word," he said. "You would not fun me around, would you?"

I had never been down the St. Lawrence Seaway—where we were headed—and only once had I met a sailor aboard a US ship who had made the Seaway trip. We used to listen to his stories and ask questions about his trip. Wouldn't the boys on the Wilson be proud of me?

We soon departed Thunder Bay for Montreal and steamed out of the harbor past the Sleeping Giant. I looked over toward Dad's house and said to myself, "What am I getting into now?"

It was time for dinner so I went to the mess room and sat down. I thought of Ernie, the first porter I had encountered. Those thoughts were interrupted by the smell of perfume and the sound of a French-accented voice whispering into my ear, "What would you like for dinner?" I turned to look, and standing beside me was the porter. I was surprised to see a woman—and a pretty one at that—aboard a ship.

Soon thereafter, it was my watch, and I was behind the wheel as *Georgian Bay* passed Isle Royale and altered course for Whitefish Point. Only three days before, I had made the crossing from Isle Royale to Houghton on the tug Colombe. Now I was on a Canadian ship heading someplace I had never been.

After the course change, I switched to automatic steering. I looked out toward the island and saw the *Ranger III* heading for Houghton on her last trip of the season. I asked the mate if I could use the radio to call the *Ranger*.

"What are you doing on the radio?" Captain Woody was surprised to hear my voice.

"I'm over here wheeling on the *Georgian Bay*," I told him. "We're headed for Montreal."

The Welland Canal

Several days later, we came to the Welland Canal at the eastern end of Lake Erie. I was fascinated. I had never seen so many locks at once. There were eight locks that bypassed Niagara Falls and took us down to the level of Lake Ontario. And Locks 4, 5, and 6 were in a row; we exited one lock immediately into the next. But there was no waiting for ships coming up the canal. These three locks were "twinned"; there were locks in both directions. Once clear of the canal and out on Lake Ontario, I realized that I had never been this far east on the water.

At the eastern end of Lake Ontario, we passed under the Thousand Islands Bridge and through the Thousand Islands. The beautiful houses—many like big castles—on the rocky islands seemed to have been built to fit. There wasn't room for much else. I learned that this is the place where Thousand Island salad dressing originated.

We were in the St. Lawrence Seaway now, and we steamed past Cornwall and Prescott, Ontario. Then came the US Seaway locks, the Eisenhower and Snell. Visitors to the locks waved at us as our ship locked through on our eastward journey.

I was on the wheel at night when we were in the South Shore Canal, a huge, winding, seemingly never-ending bend that has many rapids going around it. The banks of the canal were lit up with yellow lights located on both sides. It was the slowest and longest turn I had ever steered.

The Canadian Seaway locks ended, and we were at Montreal. With its huge buildings and illuminated skyline, the city was as beautiful at night as it was during the day. A big cathedral on top of a mountain looked down at our small ship as we quietly slid along eastward. The captain received a change of orders; we were to continue on to Quebec City.

The St. Lawrence River widened as we passed Trois-Rivières. There were many smaller villages dotted with churches along the banks. We made a pilot change, and continued toward Quebec. Just upstream from Quebec City, we passed under two bridges and the Chateau Frontenac came into view. What a marvelous sight to see such a historic building, with its spires reaching for the sky. Nearby, you could see the old town's stone walls, which were built to protect the young settlement from British invasion.

While *Georgian Bay* lay at the unloading elevator, there was plenty of time to explore. I walked up to Quebec's Old Town with its small shops and narrow cobblestone streets. There were vendors selling artwork and the smell of French cooking seeping out of the cafes where musicians played love songs. The sight of pretty French women dressed in the latest fashions from around the world was something I couldn't forget, even when I was back aboard the ship.

I got along with *Georgian Bay's* captain really well. He enjoyed hearing all about my diving experiences, especially when I'd visited shipwrecks.

"If you go to navigation school this winter and get your second mate's ticket," he told me, "I will call the office and guarantee you a mate's job aboard my ship in the spring."

"I'll think about it," I said.

"But I really would like to go back to the island in the spring."

I wasn't very interested in going back on the boats. I had made my roundtrip on the Seaway. I laid up the *Georgian Bay* in Port Colborne, Ontario, that fall and flew back to Thunder Bay.

Earning a Second Mate's Ticket

There was nothing to do over the winter months of 1974, so I decided to attend navigation school in Thunder Bay anyway. In the spring, I earned my second mate's ticket.

I waited for the National Park Service to call and let me know the date to return to fit out the tug. The call never came, and I couldn't figure out why. Surely it was time, so I packed my gear and headed for Houghton.

As I drove down the big hill overlooking the twin cities of Houghton and Hancock, Michigan, my heart sank. There in the river between the two towns was my tugboat heading back for the island without me! I rushed to the NPS office to see my boss.

I opened the door, and Charlie looked up at me like he had seen a ghost. "Dick! What are you doing here?" I could tell from Charlie's voice that something was wrong.

"I'm here to start work. Why didn't you call me?" I demanded.

We both sat down. Charlie explained that I had lost my tug job. "Last fall, when you talked to Captain Woody on the *Ranger* on his last trip, you said you were sailing on a Canadian ship. He took it to mean that you would not be coming back to the island, so he hired another skipper."

I was devastated! My world was caving in. I had lost the job of a lifetime. I drove to a spot close to the river and watched the *Colombe* pass by. "Goodbye, old girl," I said quietly, and headed back to Thunder Bay.

The Senator of Canada

○○○○○○○○○○○○○○○○○

Ship: *Senator of Canada*
Rank: Third Mate
Year: 1974

○○○○○○○○○○○○○○○○○

While I had been at navigation school in Thunder Bay, we had all heard talk of a new car ferry company that was going to start hauling railcars loaded with newsprint from Thunder Bay to Superior, Wisconsin. People at the school were excited about this new ship. They all wanted a job on her because after work they could go home every day.

A classmate, Whitey, had asked, "Are you going to fill out an application for a mate's job?"

"No, I don't think so," I had told him. "I'm new to Canada. Besides, I've never had a mate's job before." So I had held off on the application.

Now that I had lost my tug job, I found myself reconsidering. Meanwhile, Rick Hulst, a friend who sailed for N. M. Paterson &

Sons Limited, said, "I'll get you a third mate's job with Paterson if you want one."

"Okay," I said. I didn't have any other prospects at the moment.

Before I knew it, I had orders to report as third mate on the S.S. *Senator of Canada*. I was to join the ship in Toronto. I had gotten my first mate's job. I hoped I would do well.

The day before I flew to Toronto, I ran into Whitey again. "Did you ever put in your application for the car ferry job?" he asked.

Toronto, Canada today

"No, I would never get hired. Besides, I got a job with Paterson."

"Well, it wouldn't hurt to put in your application," Whitey said. "You never know, and if you got a job there, you would be in Thunder Bay all the time."

So to appease Whitey, I went to the office of Incan Ships Limited that day and gave them my application. I met a Mr. Scott, received a brief introduction to this company from England, and learned the job description. Then I left, sure that the meeting was in vain.

Aboard the Air Canada plane to Toronto the next day, the flight path took us over Isle Royale at 20,000 feet. As we flew over, I snapped all the pictures I could of the island. As the island disappeared from view, I grew lonesome. I didn't know when I would visit it again.

I sat back in my seat and soon struck up a light conversation with an older gentleman sitting next to me. After a while, I proudly announced, "I'm going to Toronto to board a ship as a new third mate."

"What ship?" the old fellow asked.

"*Senator of Canada.*"

"Well, I'm joining the same ship," he said.

"In what capacity?"

"As master," he said.

"Small world." I shrunk down into my seat a bit. Here I was, talking to this fellow, not knowing he was the captain, and I had told him I was an American and this was my first third mate's job. I didn't have any experience on the Seaway. I couldn't even read French, and all the charts down the St. Lawrence were in French. I was a greenhorn again. I thought back to my first day aboard the *Thomas Wilson* as a green deckhand when the mate said he liked greenhorns.

This time, the captain didn't say a word except for a long sigh. We didn't talk much after that.

We fit out the *Senator of Canada*, and after passing our inspection, were underway back to Thunder Bay. Most of the crew were French, so very little English was spoken. That made it very hard for me to learn my new job. I felt like I didn't belong on this ship, and before long I realized that I didn't care to be there at all.

I worked the Welland Canal with its eight locks. That was okay.

But then, on down the Seaway, I had just come on watch one night after we departed from the Iroquois Lock. I met the first mate coming off the deck, going into his room to change clothes. "Go on up to the wheelhouse," he said. "You've relieved me of the watch."

I had no sooner stepped through the wheelhouse door than the captain yelled, "What's the next course?"

The ship wasn't completely out of the lock yet, so I ran to the chart room. I had no idea where we were or even the name of the lock we were departing. I looked at the chart, and could not make out anything.

"What's the next course?" the captain yelled again. Only this time his voice sounded louder and a bit angered.

I frantically looked at the chart to find the next course but saw nothing except French. The Old Man ran to the chart as if to point out the next course; instead, he ran back out to the wheelsman. Cussing like only a sailor can, he came back to the chart room again. Not finding what he was looking for, he finally noticed that the wrong chart was laid out on top of the table. Cussing some more, he pulled open the drawer beneath the tabletop and brought out the next chart in sequence that was to be used.

"What a fine start!" I said to myself. "What happened to the nice old gentleman I met on the plane? All this carrying on, and the ship is only halfway out of the lock." Then I got angry. "He's the captain. Why does he not know the new course?" I thought.

Years later, when I was captain of another ship and departing the Iroquois Lock, I thought back to that night on the *Senator* when the first mate left me without the next set of charts laid out, and all the unnecessary screaming and cussing that took place. And the course was, and still is, 062 degrees.

Now I was sure I did not like this Old Man, his crew, and his ship. But I would stay and do my job the best I could.

A New Opportunity

On the return trip upbound in the Seaway, a thick, damp fog rolled in. Navigation on the river was closed and the Seaway ordered all vessels to proceed to the nearest anchorage and drop anchor until further notice.

We were just approaching the tie-up wall below the Snell Lock when we got the order, so we tied up on the wall to wait for the fog to clear. Once tied up, we all got off the ship and ran for the telephones to call home.

The Incan Superior; photo by Dick Metz

Finally, it was my turn to use a phone. I called my dad to find out any news.

News he had, and very good news it was.

Dad was excited. "Incan Ships called and wanted to know if you would accept the position of second officer aboard MV *Incan Superior*!"

Now I was excited, too! I almost tore the phone off the wall making a call to Mr. Scott. "Yes!" was my happy answer.

I went back aboard *Senator of Canada* and walked right up to the Old Man's room.

Without any hesitation, I told him, "I quit and will be getting off at Thunder Bay when we get back up."

Come on, fog. Let's clear up!

The Old Man was his nasty old self all the way to Thunder Bay. He tried his best to persuade me that this car ferry was nothing more than a tug and barge. "You'll regret quitting this job," he said.

On arrival in Thunder Bay, I saw the Old Man for the last, agonizing time when I went into his office to receive my discharge. "If I had known you were going to quit, I would never have taken you on as third mate."

Instead of saying that I had no idea I would get a job on the *Incan Superior*, I just turned and walked out of his office, off his ship, and away from his crew.

Once more, I was happy. The beginning of a new life and career was waiting for me.

The *Edmund Fitzgerald*; photo by Roger LeLievre

NOVEMBER 10, 1975

Ship: *Incan Superior*
Rank: First Mate
Year: 1975

We had just finished loading 26 railcars full of newsprint in Thunder Bay and were getting ready to depart the dock for Superior. By the time all the cars were chained to the deck, the northwest wind had freshened.

I checked the MAFOR (a coded marine forecast) and found that northwest gales were posted for Lake Superior. Then a special marine warning was broadcast over Channel 16, the radio channel used for distress signals, safety messages and hailing other vessels: storm warnings were up. It wasn't a night to go anywhere.

The *Incan Superior* would stay right where she was because of the approaching storm.

Some of the crewmembers who made their home in Thunder Bay went home and were to report back to the ship at midnight. I went home and returned at 2200 hours for a little rest before we got underway. When I came back aboard, I was called into the wheelhouse.

Right away, I heard the marine radio. "Calling *Edmund Fitzgerald*, calling *Edmund Fitzgerald*. Coast Guard Group Duluth calling, over."

The call was repeated. There was no answer!

I stayed on the bridge to find out why the *Fitzgerald* did not answer. After several more calls, she still didn't answer. "Must be the bad weather," I told the wheelsman. "Radio signal's not carrying very well. I'm going down to my room to take a nap."

I thought nothing more about it, because this situation had happened many times before in bad weather. The crew had all returned before their scheduled time was up. We cast off our lines and departed the safety of our dock and went out into the bay.

There were about a dozen ships that had entered the bay during the night to wait out the storm at anchor. I also noticed the *Fitzgerald* still hadn't answered the radio call.

We hauled around Angus Island and set her on course for Rock of Ages Lighthouse, some two hours distant.

Over and over, the Coast Guard called the *Fitzgerald*, but she still did not answer. Then came the most chilling announcement I ever heard in all my 30 years at sea:

"Attention, all ships. *Edmund Fitzgerald* is reported missing with all hands aboard."

I couldn't believe my ears. That was impossible in this day and age, just impossible. This couldn't happen in 1975! We all kept our ears glued to the radio that night and into the next morning. Our ship was heading for Superior, following close to the North Shore to stay protected from the wind.

After the gruesome announcement, we all sat in silence. No one said a word; each man was thinking his own thoughts. The only sounds were of the cold wind and blowing snow and seas hitting our ship's sides. As the spray washed over our deck, ice formed on the railroad cars.

"How in the world could any man launch a lifeboat in those raging seas? It would be an impossible task," I thought.

Then I said a silent prayer for each of those poor souls. "If I were out there on that storm-tossed ship without a prayer of getting into a lifeboat, what would I do?" I asked myself. "I think I would grab a bottle of vodka and head for my room and lock the door behind me."

SS EDMUND FITZGERALD
NOVEMBER 10, 1975

The sketch of the Fitzgerald wreck (from the NTSB report)

The next day, we arrived in Superior encased in blue ice. All the shore radio and television stations were broadcasting was the sinking of a ship in Lake Superior the night before. They didn't know the name of the ship that went down. There were dozens of ships on the big lake that night, and many families ashore did not know whether their loved ones were aboard the ship that had sunk. We called our company right away to tell them we were fine, and the company called the families of every one of our crew to let them know we were tied up in Superior, to their great relief.

Because of all the snow that had fallen during the storm, we could not unload or load. So that night I went down to The Main, a local sailors' hangout. I ordered a drink, and then another, and another. I could not erase from my mind what had happened. I looked up to see people dancing and singing without a care in the world. They probably didn't know that 29 men were in their ship at the bottom of Lake Superior.

After a few more drinks, I couldn't stand the feeling anymore. I walked over to the stage and up to the microphone. "Does anybody know a ship went down last night carrying its entire crew to the bottom of Lake Superior?" The music stopped and so did the dancing. You could hear a pin drop.

"Finally," I thought, "now they know, now someone cares." I asked the band to play something fitting for the *Fitzgerald* and her crew. They chose a song called "Sea of Heartbreak." I bowed my head, then walked out and returned to my ship.

Next morning, the deckhands were out on deck chopping the thick ice with axes and shoveling the broken pieces of ice over the side of the ship. The train arrived with 26 empty boxcars for our return trip. We offloaded the full cars and loaded the empties.

Then we headed back to Thunder Bay for another load. Life carried on as usual.

The *H.C. Heimbecker*; photo by James Hoffman

ABOARD THE *HEIMBECKER*

Ship: *H. C. Heimbecker*
Rank: First Mate
Year: 1980

I arrived in Thunder Bay and met Captain Bill Smith aboard the *Heimbecker* in November 1980. It was snowing, and ice was starting to accumulate in the bays as the *Heimbecker* departed for Owen Sound, Ontario, on Lake Huron.

Bill was a fine gentleman, and a veteran of many years on the lakes. He was to retire once we were tied up in Owen Sound. In the meantime, on the way there, I picked his brain for all I could learn about everything, and I mean everything. He told me many useful things about weather, about where to go in a storm, and also about where not to go.

Smelling the Weather

I have never met a man who knew weather like he did. He could smell the air and tell what kind of weather was about to happen. He told me, "Sonny, make love to that North Shore of Superior. It will be your best friend in storms. Don't take the 'Old Girl' out into anything. She is old and needs a rest."

We had crossed Lake Superior and were just about to the Soo Locks, and I was thinking that we should be up to the wheelhouse by now. I was getting kind of jumpy. "Cap," I said, "shouldn't we be up on the bridge now?"

"No," he said. "Let the mates take it. That's what they get paid for. Bill Parker, Roy Hooper and Fern, they've been on here for years. Don't ever worry about those boys."

The captain's office on the Heimbecker, photo by Dick Metz

Finally, as the ship was sliding the wall leading to the MacArthur Lock, old Captain Bill went up to the pilothouse and inched the *Heimbecker* into the lock. The gates closed, the water level dropped. One short blast of the old steam whistle, the lines came off, and out of the lock we went. Down to his room the captain went. "Let the mates take over. That's what they get paid for," he said again.

We arrived in Owen Sound, and I knew Captain Bill was not in a hurry to get off the ship.

I didn't see any bags packed, and he hadn't said a word to me about when he was going to go. All this time, I had been sleeping (or trying to) on a short couch with my legs hanging over the sides. I hadn't slept much since coming aboard in Thunder Bay.

Bill had been nice to me and treated me as his equal. I didn't have the heart to ask him anything about leaving or about when I could unpack my gear and get some sleep. I slept on that short couch again that night. The next day, I thought I would get a hotel room for the night. I went downtown to look around for a few hours. When I returned to the *Heimbecker*, to my surprise, Captain Bill Smith was gone. We never met again, and I finally slept in a real bed.

A New Captain on the Lakes

Ship: *H. C. Heimbecker*
Rank: Captain
Year: 1980

The weather was getting colder, and the ice in Owen Sound's harbor was a few inches thick. Our grain cargo had been unloaded, and we were ready to back the ship up, and with the help of the winch on the bow, pull the ship away from the dock.

It was easy to do, if you had done this sort of maneuver previously. This was my first time at ship handling, and I was chomping at the bit to do it. I started to use the engine to kick the stern away from the dock, but the ice held fast. We moved back and forth, up and down the wall to break up the ice. Finally, she started to turn and when she cleared the end of the wall I rang up full ahead. Out through the piers we went.

As we sailed, I thought to myself, "Here's the scenario: a new captain sailing amid the November gales on an old, slow ship. Lake Superior, here we come, and may God bless us."

The *Heimbecker* underway; photo by Dick Metz

MY FIRST SHIP AS CAPTAIN

Ship: *H. C. Heimbecker*
Rank: Captain
Year: 1980

The *H. C. Heimbecker* was built in 1905. At 569 feet long, she had been considered large at one time, but for a vessel operating in 1980, she was a small ship. Her quarters and pilothouse were small, too. Between the captain, the mate and the wheelsman in the pilothouse, it got crowded in the pilothouse. In rough weather, when spray froze on the pilothouse windows, you couldn't see out unless a heater was installed next to the glass to melt the ice.

The captain's quarters fared no better in terms of room, but it was very cozy. The master gyrocompass, which was used to instantly determine direction—was located close to my bed, and all night long I heard the whining noise of the gyro spinning and blue lights flashing off the overhead (ceiling). The bulkheads were oak, and in my office was an old rolltop desk. Small as she was, it was home.

Too Much Speed

Shortly after we departed Owen Sound, the Coast Guard posted gale warnings blowing from the north. The *Heimbecker* was slow, and I figured by the time we arrived at Cove Island, the gale might blow itself out. If it didn't, I would hold close to the North Shore of Lake Huron. We got lucky, and at Cove Island the gale warnings were discontinued, so I set course for DeTour Village, Michigan.

We had a nice run across Lake Huron and up the St. Marys River. I felt very confident with my new job, maybe a bit too confident. We came around Mission Point, and I called the Lockmaster to report our position.

He said, "Upbound on the Mac Lock. The lock is clear." That was good news for me.

As I pulled alongside the old power plant at Sault Ste. Marie, Michigan, the first mate said, "Cap, you still have her going full ahead."

I didn't want the mate to know that I made a mistake by not slowing down sooner, so I just rang up dead slow ahead and hoped and prayed she would slow down enough to make the wall below the lock. It worked, as she slid right up to the wall and into the lock.

From that day on, I never again forgot to check her speed down.

Should Have Called for a Tugboat

We had a good run across Lake Superior, and when we got to Thunder Cape, near Thunder Bay, Lake Shippers called with our orders: Go to McCabe's Elevator to load. There was a salty (an ocean-going ship) loading at Pool #1.

The wind had freshened some from the south, and we entered the bay. The wind was getting stronger by the minute. Just before we got to the piers, I picked up my field glasses and looked at the big salty tied up on the opposite side of our slip, loading grain.

Thunder Bay from Mt. McKay

"It's blowing a bit stiff on our port side," the mate said over the radio from his position on deck. "Did we order a tug?"

"No, I don't need a tug," I said, still beaming with confidence. "Steer on the stern of that salty," I instructed the wheelsman. "We'll keep the ship upwind, and when we get closer, let her fall to starboard and into the slip."

We headed on the salty's stern at slow speed, and at the right time, I let her fall off to starboard. I let her fall a little too much and could not bring her back, and the starboard bow came up on the wall with a little bump. I thought to myself, "Great job, Captain," and thought about the money I had saved the company by not using a tug.

After we tied up, the first mate called me on the radio. "I'm going to get the chief. Can you meet us on the dock?"

I met the mate and the chief at the ladder. "What do you want?" I asked.

"We came up hard on the corner of the wall," he said. "There may be damage to the ship."

"I didn't feel any bump," the chief said.

I agreed with the chief, but of course, I would agree.

The three of us walked forward to where a deckhand stood pointing to the hull. I could not believe my eyes! The hull plating was stove in (dented) about eight inches wide and about ten feet long. I felt really sick; all my confidence was shot right then and there.

I called the office and sheepishly told Captain Dean what had happened. The ship was inspected, and after a little welding by the chief, we were given permission to load.

That was the first and last time I didn't use a tugboat when I needed one.

The *Heimbecker* amid the ice in Georgian Bay; photo by Dick Metz

THE LONGEST TRIP

○○○○○○○○○○○○○○○○○

Ship: *H. C. Heimbecker*
Rank: Captain
Year: 1980

○○○○○○○○○○○○○○○○○

Author's note: *Most trips on the Great Lakes take a matter of three days or so. This trip took 11 days because of a combination of rough weather, ice, and having to anchor.*

My longest trip ever started in November aboard the *H. C. Heimbecker*. We cast off our lines and departed Owen Sound for Superior, Wisconsin, for a load of grain. Gale warnings were up when we left.

When we got to Cove Island, the storm didn't die down; instead, it increased and soon there were storm warnings with winds out of the northwest.

I tried to anchor the old girl behind Cove Island, but it was too rough for a good anchorage. The wind and sea came around both ends of the small island and met right where we had attempted to anchor. I decided to pull up the anchor and try to drop it elsewhere in a more favorable place. When the mate tried to raise the anchor, it would not come up. It was caught on the rocks below. We tried different things, but she was caught tightly.

"Now what?" I thought. "Cut the chain?" If all else failed, we could cut it off, because we couldn't stay here. I would give it one more try and see what happened. Forward I went until the chain was leading astern, at which point I rang up full astern, and she started to back and gather speed. When the chain came out of the water, it was as tight as a guitar string. The anchor snapped loose from the rocks and the mate heaved it up. There was no damage and we put the anchor in its pocket on the side of the ship.

Finding a Spot to Anchor

After studying the charts for a suitable place to re-anchor, I decided to backtrack around the point and anchor at Dyer Bay. The water was very deep right offshore, so we had to go in close to the beach to drop the anchor. We sat there at anchor for two days.

I decided to try to sneak along the North Shore of Georgian Bay because the wind was veering to the north and there was still a big sea out on Lake Huron. We followed our charted course around and in between the many small, scattered islands that dot the north side of the bay.

That day, it started snowing, and the snow was thick. We came to the end of the shelter from the friendly islands, and we ventured out into the big lake, still hugging the shore to the north, which helped protect us from the wind somewhat.

The next day, the little *Heimbecker*, snow-covered and belching black smoke from her funnel, came into view of DeTour. At anchor in the bay there were quite a few ships, waiting out the storm just as we did. The skipper of a 1000-footer called on the radio to ask me what kind of weather we had out on Lake Huron. I told him of our route, and felt mighty proud of our little ship as we sailed past all the "big boys."

After our trip up the St. Marys River, we departed the Soo Locks and headed across Lake Superior, just as the easterly gale warning went up. We veered to the northeast at this point. The mate and I plotted a course for the North Shore of the lake, again to take advantage of some shelter from the wind. We

At the Soo Locks today

reduced our speed to half, and planned that when the wind shifted to the northeast, we would alter course for Copper Harbor.

I went to lie down for a rest, but I couldn't fall asleep. I kept looking out my porthole, noting the wind's direction by observing the smoke from the stack. It continued to blow from the east, and after a while, I finally went to sleep. For the moment, we were riding well.

When I awoke, I checked the stack again. The smoke was blowing right up the deck. I glanced at the hissing, glowing master gyrocompass next to my bed, and it showed that we were on a course for Copper Harbor. I went up the bridge for a chat with the mate and a cup of steaming hot coffee.

Another Course Change

At this point, I checked the latest marine forecast, which indicated that the gales would return to a westerly direction. My new plan was to keep on this course toward Copper Harbor, and when the wind turned westerly, we would head west for Minnesota's North Shore. Once we got close, we would head toward Superior, Wisconsin. The mate and I talked over the new plan, and we both agreed it was the best course of action.

I returned to bed, right next to the humming master gyro. I fell asleep within no time at all. I had finally gotten used to the gyro.

I awoke to the sound of my ship's phone ringing. "Wind's out of the west," said the mate. "We're in mid-lake, and she's riding good, so I'll keep her on this course. When she starts to roll, we steer west."

"Okay with me," I said, and went back to sleep.

When the ship started rolling, I woke up and went up to the wheelhouse. I nodded to the mate, and he gave the wheelsman the order to steer a course of west. Again, she settled down and was riding well on her new westerly heading. "I hope this is the last of the gales coming from every direction of the compass," I thought. But that was not the case.

More Gales

This time, the gales came from the southeast. And again we were on the wrong side of the lake for a southeast wind.

Again we altered course. This time we steered for the Apostle Islands. When parallel of Devils Island Light, we altered course for Superior's piers. We were safely in the corner of the lake where no change of wind could harm us except for a blow from the north. "Don't even think about that possibility," I told myself.

Well, we made it safely to our elevator, tied up, and began loading grain. I left the ship for a while and walked downtown. I walked past the local sailors' bar—The Main—and thought of what had happened the last time that I was here. It had been the night the *Edmund Fitzgerald* went down. (See page 75.) I didn't stop, but continued to walk to the Hammond Steak House next to the High Bridge. I treated myself to a martini along with the biggest T-bone that they had on the menu.

Northeast Gales and Sea Smoke

The weather got colder, and thick ice formed in our slip around the ship's hull. The next day, we departed the Superior elevator with two tugs assisting us. Northwest gales were still up. We turned and headed for the Duluth entry to the port. I called the Aerial Lift Bridge to check for inbound traffic, and we were given the okay to go under the bridge.

Because of the northwest gale, I decided to follow Minnesota's North Shore, and we headed for Thunder Bay. The lake was still quite ruffled up because of the recent gales from each point of the compass. As we passed Silver Bay, Minnesota, sea smoke covered the lake near us with cold columns of fog that took on eerie forms, which danced on the water and spiraled upwards. I felt like we were in another world.

At Thunder Bay

As the gales raged on, there was no sense battling the elements when there was shelter nearby, so we steamed into Thunder Bay and dropped our anchor. It was becoming almost shiny from all the use it was getting. We waited out the gale close to the main breakwall.

We had neighbors in the bay; other skippers had the same idea about waiting out the gale.

Next morning, the mate called, "The other ships are getting underway, Cap. Should I call the engine room to warm up the engine?"

Whitefish Point on a NOAA Chart

"No, we will wait till afternoon," I replied. "When the marine forecast comes out, then we will make our decision."

The noon forecast looked good, so we lifted up our well-used anchor and slowly proceeded down the lake. At Passage Island, we altered our course for Whitefish Point.

We had a following sea (the waves were following our direction) and a good ride across the big lake.

We rounded Whitefish Point, and when parallel to Ile Parisienne, we called in to the Soo. We were advised that because of all the ice around the lock, we would have to anchor until further notice. I picked a good spot off Iroquois Point, and put our well-used anchor down again.

Now, one by one, the same ships that were at anchor with me up in Thunder Bay began arriving and dropping their hooks. We were already anchored, and they were just now arriving. Most had taken a course around the North Shore, but some had turned around and anchored at Thunder Bay until the lake calmed down. They had all been in a hurry to go. Once the first ship departed, they all followed suit and got underway, only to find out that the lake was too rough to cross, and they were burning up fuel in the process. On the other hand, we had lain at anchor a little longer in a nice, quiet bay, having been the last to depart and had a nice run across the center of the lake. We arrived without burning extra fuel. I used that same method for years afterward, and it usually worked out well for me.

A Parking Lot at the Locks

The next morning, I saw ships anchored everywhere. The US Coast Guard formed a convoy of ships to proceed down to the lock. *Heimbecker* was the first ship leading the convoy. The number two ship behind me was the 858-foot *Roger Blough*. The trip down toward the lock went very slowly. Several times, we got stuck in the ice and had to call for assistance from the Coast Guard. Finally, we arrived at the lock.

The lockmaster had all sorts of trouble with ice jamming the lock gates. Once we got tied up inside the lock, he had trouble trying to close the gate behind us.

Once we got through, we were in the ice again. The ice got thicker, and before we got to Mission Point, the *Heimbecker* had come to a halt in the ice. The old girl could not move one inch in either direction. Again, the Coast Guard icebreaker broke us loose and attempted to break a trail for us to follow. But the pressure of the ice and the wind kept us in a tight grip.

Because of thick ice in the Rock Cut and Moon Island Cut—both vital parts of the trip through the St. Marys River—the Coast Guard closed the downbound channel (the one for ships heading away from Lake Superior). The downbound vessels had to use the upbound channel, and this created a bottleneck. The upbound vessels had to wait at anchor until all the downbound ships cleared the buoy.

All the while, the *Roger Blough* was still behind us. Each time we got stuck, the *Blough* would come right up behind our stern and stop until we could move again. Hour after hour, this game replayed itself. I thought that by this time the captain of the *Blough* was probably getting tired of this, so I called him on the radio. "Would you like to go by me?"

"No, thanks," he responded. "You're doing a good job."

I guess the *Heimbecker* was his private icebreaker!

Dropping Anchor Again

Another boat in our fleet, the *Robert S. Pierson*, was about six hours ahead of us, and Captain Larry went to anchor below Lime Island for the night. He had had enough for one day.

"I've had enough, too," I thought. "When I get this ship down where *Robert S.* is, I'll call it a day." I had also had enough ice for one day. It had been stop-and-go all the way. When I saw the *Robert S.* ahead, I closed up right under his stern and dropped our trusty old anchor one more time.

I gave Larry a call. "Let me know when you're ready to depart in the morning," I said. I was asleep before my head hit the pillow, a well-deserved rest.

The *Robert S. Pierson*; photo by James Hoffman

Only a few hours later it was morning, and my phone rang. Larry was all bright and shiny and raring to go. I really wasn't ready yet, but I got up nonetheless.

Robert S. Pierson had lots of power and great speed. After the engine warmed up, he broke a trail for me, and I stayed right on his stern all the way to DeTour and into the open waters of Lake Huron.

I thanked Captain Larry, as the *Robert S.* belched a big puff of black smoke from her stack. I soon lost sight of the ship over the horizon. I thought about what great speed she had. My ship was slow, but she was steady, and as the start-again, stop-again voyage through the gales had proven, she got the job done.

The *Soo River Trader*; photo by Dick Metz

NEW CAPTAIN, OLD SHIP, NOVEMBER GALES

Ship: *Soo River Trader*
Rank: Second Captain
Year: 1980

When I left the *Incan Superior* in the fall of 1980, I flew to Toronto. From there, I took a taxi to the office of the Soo River Company located in Thorold, Ontario. The office was inside a neat little white house situated next to Lock 7 Motel.

I met Captain Ron Dean, and he introduced me to Mr. Robert Pierson. I liked everybody from the start. It was a family atmosphere, and that atmosphere would last for 20 years. In many shipping companies, employees are nothing more than their employee number. Not so with *Soo River*. You were treated like family.

I was surprised that Robert Pierson was so young; after all, he owned a shipping company. And he was not the least bit high-headed. He was a regular guy, a nice guy.

Dinner was with Captain Dean. We talked about the company, and he told me I would go aboard the *E. J. Newberry* as second captain (a Captain in Training), since I hadn't been down the Seaway in years. That was quite all right with me.

After dinner, Captain Dean shook my hand. "Good luck." I didn't sleep very well in my room at Lock 7 Motel that night. I thought back to the night just before I joined my first ship, the *Thomas Wilson*. I didn't sleep very well that night either. "Here we go again," I thought. "What will happen this time?"

Before I knew it, the alarm clock was blaring. Time to go. At 3 a.m., my eyes barely open, I was standing next to the guard shack as the bow of the *Newberry* inched her way into Lock 7 of the Welland Canal. Once aboard, I met Captain Jerry Bissette, and my career started all over again.

The E.J. Newberry; photo by James Hoffman

Everything proceeded nicely aboard the *Newberry*. I was learning how she handled and we made the Seaway trip a few times. After about two months, in the black of night, Captain Bissette turned and said, "You take her through the Brockville Narrows yourself this time."

"Cap, I don't think I am ready to be turned loose by myself yet," I protested.

"Well, I am going to bed. She's all yours." Off to bed he went.

I certainly felt lonely in the quiet of the wheelhouse. Of course, I would not dare show my fear in front of the wheelsman. I was thankful that it was dark inside the wheelhouse. He couldn't see my knees knocking together.

I walked up to look out the front window. All I saw was a mess of red and green blinking lights as far as my eye could see. How in the world could I go in between all those flashing lights? They were everywhere. Beads of sweat formed on my brow. "God, I am in command!" I thought.

The bow was before the first set of navigational lights. On the waterways of the Great Lakes, there are many lighted navigational lights that help sailors stay in the shipping lanes. The lights, which are green or red, mark the shipping channel, and when you're returning to port, the rule of thumb is *red, right, return*—keep the red buoy on the right.

"Okay, red, right, return," I said to myself. The red flashing light passed off the starboard bow, and the green was off to port. "Made it!" I thought, as the next pair came close. "Okay, now do the same thing again. And again. Heck, this is all right." I just kept taking the first two ahead of me and keeping the ship between them. Soon, I started feeling pretty good about what I was doing. But the feeling did not last very long.

"Downbound, Brockville Narrows in 30 minutes," came the security call over the radio.

"Oh, no!" I thought. I had never met a ship in the narrows, not even in the daytime. It was risky business to meet another ship there. "What should I do? Call the captain? Try to beat the other ship through? What if I try and don't beat him?" Panic was setting in.

Then I heard a calm voice over the radio. "Good morning, Captain. Where about are you?"

I tried not to let the fright show in my voice when I replied. "Just below McNair Island," I managed to gurgle out.

"Oh," came the calm voice, "in that case, we will be through the Narrows in time to meet you below Skeleton Island."

Those words were beautiful. And he was right where he said he would be as we passed in the night. I glanced at my wheelsman, expecting to see horror on his face, but he just stood there humming an unrecognizable tune, without a worry in the world. He didn't know how much I had suffered. Really, I would have never left me in charge of the bridge that night, or any other night, until I had gained more experience.

Captain Bissette went on holiday, and Captain Percy was placed in command. He was a much older man. I don't think he was very impressed with me at first. I guess we got off on the wrong foot when he asked me where the key for the safe was located.

"In the safe," I said. "It's never locked."

"Well, it is now; I just locked it."

I started laughing, quietly, but he heard it. That was it for me.

Thirty days later, when Captain Bissette came back, I asked Captain Percy if he would put a good word into the office for me so I could sail my own ship.

"No," was his answer. "I will not put in a good word for you because you will never make a good captain."

I was shocked by his answer. Wow! I was really sorry then for laughing over that safe key affair. He never did call the company for me.

We were all glad to have Captain Bissette back. "How did things go with Percy?" he asked me.

I told him exactly what had happened, and I included how he said I'd never sail my own boat and would not make a good captain.

The H. C. Heimbecker; photo by Dick Metz

Captain Bissette grunted, walked over to his desk, and called the company's office. "I'd like to speak with Captain Dean," he said. "Ron, this is Jerry. Do you have a boat for Dick to sail? He is ready to be cut loose and should have been weeks ago." There was a pause, and Jerry handed me the phone.

"Get off in the Welland Canal upbound and fly to Thunder Bay," Captain Dean told me. "When you get there, join the *H. C. Heimbecker* as master."

Needless to say, thank you, Captain Jerry Bissette.

The *Soo River Trader*; photo by James Hoffman

A SHORT TOOT

Ship: Steamer *Soo River Trader*
Rank: Captain
Year: 1981

In April 1981, I received my orders to report aboard the *Soo River Trader* in Toronto, where she had been laid up for the winter. I pulled up to the ship in a taxi and got a good look at her for the first time.

She was old and looked somewhat beat-up from the weather, but I could see that she had good lines. It would take some cleaning up and lots of paint, but she could look pretty good again.

As I stood there looking up at her rusting old hull, I thought back to the day when I was sitting in the pilothouse on the *Incan Superior*, which was only one year old at the time.

While I sat there, I saw the *Soo River Trader* (then known as the *Goderich*) depart the Kam River in Thunder Bay. As she passed by, I turned to the wheelsman, "How can they get men to sail on an old rust bucket like that?" I noticed her small cabins and galley area, and thought, "I'm glad I'll never have to sail on a ship like her."

The wheelsman made a comment that I never forgot. "When you are on a slow ship like that, you only make half of the trips that a faster ship makes per year. It also means making only half the number of locks. You never have to worry about checking her down for speed, and you get the same pay as a man sailing a new and faster ship, and he would be doing twice the work."

I gave this some thought and said, "No, I don't want anything like that."

Ironically, now here I was going aboard that old ship.

None of the forward crew was aboard yet, so I went to my cabin to have a look around. At least she was better and bigger than the *Heimbecker*. My captain's quarters were not that bad. I laid my bags on the couch and looked at my desk. There were several dirty glasses stuck to the desktop; they had sat there all winter. There were also a few empty booze and beer bottles. Someone must have been glad to lay up; there must have been a party.

I walked aft to the galley and met our chief cook, Glenna Loughridge. She offered me a hot cup of coffee, and I took an instant liking to her. It was the beginning of a friendship that lasted over 20 years.

Heading Out

In the morning, I signed on the rest of the crew and we readied the ship. The following day, we had our inspection, and the chief engineer said he would have the engines ready to go that evening.

Around midnight, my phone rang. The mate was on the other end. "Cap, the engine's ready and the deckhands are standing by on the dock."

I went up to the pilothouse and told the mate, "When I blow a short toot from the whistle, let go of the lines and get your men aboard." When everything was ready, I reached for the whistle handle and gave it a quick jerk, fully expecting a short toot. The short toot got longer and longer; the whistle would not stop blowing. "Hang onto her," I told the mate. The whistle kept on blowing until the steam ran out. I didn't have to call the chief; he knew what had happened.

The engineers tinkered, and a few hours later, we tried it all over again. This time, I got my short toot and the boys cut her loose. I started to back her down the dock. We got three ship lengths when the chief called. "We lost the boiler." So we had to tie her up again.

A Broken Boiler

Those not working on the problem went to bed. The next morning, the chief reported to me, "The boiler is shot. We can't sail until it's fixed."

It was left to me to call the company and give them the bad news. I did just that. Later in the afternoon, the office wanted to know if I could take her over to Hamilton on one boiler for repairs. We did, and after she was safely tied up at our berth in Hamilton, I sent the forward end crew home until she would be ready to sail.

Repairs couldn't be made in Hamilton, so with the aid of three tugs, the *Trader* was towed to Port Colborne.

While we were there, I was in my room watching television when I was startled by a knock at my door. I was the only person aboard, or so I thought. I cautiously answered the door and there was Captain Bob Welland, one of the last of the old-time lake skippers.

Many Questions

We talked about a lot of things, but mostly I asked lots of questions. I had questions about sailing a ship and questions about how to get into specific ports. My main concern was how to make the piers at Port Colborne during a southwest gale. I had heard horror stories about trying to enter Port Colborne in a storm.

He said, "You don't! But, if you do get caught on the lake during a southwest gale, this is what you do. First thing is to line up the big smokestack from the old nickel plant with the east breakwall light and keep them in line till you are a half-mile from the piers. Then let her drift down to the green buoy until the piers line up. Go full ahead and hard port (left) wheel, and in you go."

I wrote every word down and drew a sketch of the plan. "That's the way to do it!" Bob said.

He also gave me some advice that I went by for my entire career. "Do not be in a hurry. When you think you are going too slow ahead, put her full astern! Do not put your vessel out into any danger. If you are not sure, go to anchor."

We talked for hours, and I took many valuable notes. Later, I passed these notes along to many mates as they progressed in their careers toward becoming a captain.

Repairs and New Paint

The boiler repairs in Port Colborne took a few weeks. During that time, we had "Soo River Company" painted on the ship's sides, along with a white stripe around the bow and stern—the Soo River colors. The old girl looked great displaying her new paint job.

Soo River Trader; photo by Dick Metz

In fact, she was one of the nicest-looking ships on the Great Lakes. All season, small craft and other ships would call on the radio to tell us what a fine-looking ship we had. I think the *Trader* was Mr. Pierson's favorite ship. (He was the President of the Soo River Company.) We were all proud of the old girl.

Anyway, with a full crew back aboard and the engine warmed up, I gave that small toot once more, and we backed away from our berth. As we backed away, the third mate, who was stationed in the back of the boat, was trying to tell me something over the radio.

But he had a speech problem, and I could not understand what he was trying to tell me. I got the ship turned for Lock 8 of the Welland Canal and rang up slow ahead. As we entered the lock, the third mate kept right on talking, and still wasn't making any sense. We departed Lock 8 without needing to tie up (the elevation shift isn't very pronounced on this lock), and we headed toward the piers into Lake Erie.

The third mate came up to the bridge huffing and puffing and tried to tell me something. Finally, he got it out, and I understood. "Cap, when we left the dock, the stern wire got caught on the dock, and I could not get it off. When we started forward, the wire started paying off the winch. When it came to the end, it flopped into the water! The whole wire came off the drum, and it's on the bottom of the canal." This was what he had been trying to tell me, but in his excitement, he could not express himself.

"This is going to be some season!" I thought.

On the present-day Welland Canal

A Worn-Out Ship

On each trip, before entering Hamilton, I had the crew paint over the scratches on her sides from all of the locks we had to make. But, as nice as she looked, the Trader was old and her machinery was worn out. Without warning, her anchors would even drop by themselves!

On one trip through the Seaway, we were about to proceed into St. Lambert Lock, and with a thundering crash and without any notice at all, the anchor decided to let go. It dropped out of its pocket and into the canal with all 700 feet of anchor chain behind it.

So we heaved it back up.

While we were heaving the anchor, the Seaway called and wanted to know why we dropped the anchor.

"It was a mistake," I told the lockmaster. "The watchman dropped it by mistake due to a lack of communication between the bridge and the deck."

He didn't seem very impressed with my answer. But if I had told the lockmaster the truth about the anchor dropping on its own, he would have held the ship up until repairs were made. Then there would have been an inspection with a bunch of paperwork to follow. (It was better to fib once in a while.) But I did get the chief to rig something up to keep her from dropping.

Engine Failures Abound

The first engine failure we had underway happened one foggy morning. We crept into the MacArthur Lock heading upbound (away from the Atlantic). The lockmaster asked if I wanted to sign a release form to depart the lock in fog.

"Yes, I will," I said. I signed the form, and we left the lock in thick fog.

Abeam of Big Point above the Soo Locks, the engine broke down, and we went to anchor. I called Soo Control, told them what happened and gave our position. The chief and his gang worked feverishly all night to repair the engine, but to no avail.

When the fog cleared the next morning, we were anchored right in the center of the river where we would be blocking all upbound and downbound ships. Soo Control called and said I had to move out of the main channel because were blocking traffic. So I called a tug company from the Soo, and two tugs came out and towed the Trader out of the main channel.

The next day, the chief finished all the necessary repairs, and we got underway for Thunder Bay.

Before the season was over, we had so many engine failures that when we stopped, I wouldn't even call the poor chief. We both knew what to do. Fortunately, the engine never failed in a narrow river channel where we might have gone aground.

The *H.C. Heimbecker*, Christmas 1980; photo by Dick Metz

SILENT NIGHT

Ship: *H. C. Heimbecker*
Rank: Captain
Year: 1980

Just before Christmas in 1980, I received reports from the company office that Georgian Bay was completely covered with ice. The only vessel moving there was the *John E. F. Misener*, which was a few hours ahead of us on the *H. C. Heimbecker*. Like us, it was also heading for Midland, Ontario. If we could find and follow her track, we would have a better chance of not getting stuck in the ice.

We picked up her track and played follow the leader. I knew that if we got stuck out there, the ship would stay right where she was until the spring. But the day was bright with blue sky from horizon to horizon. The track was visible, and we plowed through the broken ice.

Off in the distance, I saw four deer running across the ice. I did not want them to plunge through the broken ice of our track and not be able to climb back out, so I blew a long blast from our ship's whistle. The deer were within about 20 feet of falling in, but they spread their front legs and put on the brakes. As they slid to a stop, their long ears flopped in front of their faces. They heard that old steam whistle blowing, sniffed the air, turned around and headed back to shore. It was a good day.

Arriving at Midland

We arrived at Midland, and the *John Misener* was unloading at the elevator where we were to unload. There was no room at the dock for us to tie up to wait, so we stopped the ship just outside of the elevator and let her freeze in the ice. After the *Misener* discharged her cargo, we planned to wrest her free of the ice and move her under the unloading leg. Until then, we were frozen in.

On December 25, 1980, frozen solid in the ice a half-mile out from shore, the crew of the *H. C. Heimbecker* celebrated Christmas. The galley staff prepared a wonderful feast. We had prime rib, roast duck, and all the delicious trimmings that went along with it, plus an assortment of cakes and candies. Of course, most of the crew would rather have been celebrating Christmas with their loved ones at home, but that's the life of a sailor on the Great Lakes.

After dinner, the crew left the galley and went to their cabins to read or watch TV. The men on watch went back to the pilothouse or engine room to finish standing their watch. The Chief and I sat for a while talking about all the years that we never made it home for Christmas. We just went along with it; this was our job and a way of life, but a few of the younger crewmembers were very homesick. I believe that if the ship had been tied up to the dock, some of the deckhands would have quit and gone home.

I said good night to the chief and thanked the galley crew for an excellent dinner, and I started up the deck to my cabin. The snow had stopped falling and I could hear the fresh snow crackling under my feet as I walked up the steel deck. I could smell the pure cold air, and I could smell the smoke from the wood-burning fireplaces from the houses on shore, the smoke slowing rising into the quiet air from the chimneys. It was a beautiful night, so I walked up to the bow and looked at all the pretty twinkling Christmas lights that most of the homes were displaying. A good feeling came over me and I realized how lucky I was to be out here this Christmas night, a truly silent night on a ship that was iced in a half-mile from shore and so far from home and family.

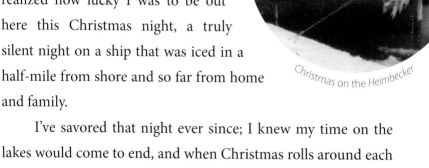

Christmas on the Heimbecker

I've savored that night ever since; I knew my time on the lakes would come to end, and when Christmas rolls around each year, I find myself thinking of that silent scene, and the smells and feelings that came with it.

The *Misener* finished unloading the next day. The crew moved their ship to the end of the wall and secured it for the winter. The crew was paid, and they all went home. On the 28th of December, we were unloaded and tied up alongside of the *Misener*. After laying up the ship for the winter, I paid off the crew, except for the engineers, who still had some work to finish quieting the steam plant for the winter. Everybody happily went home for a well-deserved rest and to spend what was left of Christmas with their families.

The *Judith M. Pierson*; photo by Bob Campbell

SHORE LEAVES

○-○-○-○-○-○-○-○-○-○-○-○-○-○-○-○

Ship: *Judith M. Pierson*
Rank: Captain
Year: 1982

○-○-○-○-○-○-○-○-○-○-○-○-○-○-○-○

Author's note: The following stories are some of the more notable shore leaves from my career.

It took several days to unload the *Judith M. Pierson* at Quebec City, so I decided to have a good look at this quaint little old French town with its narrow cobblestone streets dotted with outdoor cafes and wandering minstrels.

Most of the French women were beautiful, each trying to out-dress each other in the latest fashions from Paris.

I walked up the steep hill to the Chateau Frontenac. The huge, greenish chateau's copper roof had many spires, all reaching for the sky. What an impressive sight, situated on the high cliffs overlooking the mighty St. Lawrence River.

Later that evening, I stopped for a fine French dinner at the Chateau. I washed it down with a flask of French wine, and then went into the lounge to sip an after-dinner drink. Two lovely French girls walked in and ordered drinks. A little bit later, I walked over and introduced myself and sat down for a conversation. I quickly found out that we were not doing very well; I did not speak a word of their native tongue, nor did they speak mine. It was fun trying to guess what we were all trying to say, and we laughed about it. I was getting nowhere fast with this approach, however, until my first mate, Didier, walked in.

We used Didier as our interpreter, and soon we were having fun drinking and dancing. I spent the entire weekend with one of the beautiful French girls. She showed me all around Quebec City. There were many lovely parks with beautiful flowers, and we enjoyed wine at several outdoor cafes. Life was beautiful.

Of course, she spoke French, and I, English. But I have never forgotten that weekend in Quebec City.

○○○○○○○○○○○○○○○○○○

Ship: *Thomas Wilson*
Rank: Deckhand
Year: 1964

○○○○○○○○○○○○○○○○○○

It was my first trip aboard a freighter as a deckhand, and by the time we got to Cleveland, I felt like I had been at sea for years instead of only two and a half days. The mate let us off work. "Be back aboard at midnight," he admonished us.

We strolled uptown together. It sure felt good to be on land where it was warm.

As sailors often do, we walked into the first bar we came to. The barmaid was dressed in a very flimsy outfit, and we didn't mind—she looked good.

A visit, a song, and a lifelong memory

After a few rounds of drinks, I got up to play the jukebox, and the barmaid said, "Play the 'French Song,' by Lucille Starr."

I played that song, and it has stuck with me for more than 37 years. Today, when I hear the "French Song" by Lucille Starr, I think back to the day when I was green and visited that Cleveland bar with the other deckhands.

○-○-○-○-○-○-○-○-○-○-○-○-○-○-○-○

Ship: *Judith M. Pierson*
Rank: Captain
Year: 1982

○-○-○-○-○-○-○-○-○-○-○-○-○-○-○-○

When I left the ship, I told the cook that I would not be back for dinner. I was planning to have the best prime rib at the Twine House, located just across the river from where *Judith M. Pierson* was loading.

First Mate Didier was in charge of the loading. "I'm having dinner at the Twine House," I told him. "If I'm not back one hour before we're done loading, shine the stern spotlight across the harbor and into the windows of the restaurant over there."

This would be my signal to return quickly because we were just about loaded.

During the course of my dinner at the Twine House, I met a lot of people. When they found out that I was the captain of the *Judy* and my plan for signaling completion of loading, everybody waited for the spotlight to be turned on.

I was occupied on the dance floor, and the bandleader said, "Not to worry, Captain. We will watch for the light."

A short time later, a big roar went up from the people in the restaurant. "There is your light, Cap."

I thanked everybody and told them that in appreciation for their kindness, I would blow a salute from the steam whistle when we departed. There was applause and another cheer went up. I hustled back to the ship.

The *Judith M. Pierson*; photo by Dick Metz

The deckhands let go of the lines and scrambled up the ladder. I rang up half astern. When I got the *Judy* straightened around and heading out, I blew a long Master's salute, to the delight of the crowd, which was shouting and waving goodbye.

I laid up the *Judith M. Pierson* at Toronto on December 30, 1982. My friend, Captain Rick Hulst, had laid up the *Joseph X. Robert* at Toronto the day before. I had my airplane ticket to fly home to Florida on December 31. Rick wanted me to spend the weekend in Toronto, but I told him no; I was tired of the cold weather and wanted to fly to Florida.

Now, the Soo River Company had just bought a new uniform for me, so I thought I would wear it home, since I didn't have room to pack it in my luggage.

December 31 was a cold, windy day in Toronto. It was snowing when we took off, and I watched the city disappear into the snow. "How nice it is going to be to see the warm sun in just a few hours," I thought.

In Atlanta, I changed planes and departed for Melbourne, Florida. As it happened, I was the only passenger on the entire flight. Seeing me sitting alone there in my uniform, the stewardess asked, "Would you like to sit up in first class?"

Of course, I did. Four stewardesses sat around me and offered me drinks. I had several drinks during the hour-and-a-half flight and thought it was pretty good to have free drinks. I figured it was because it was New Year's Eve.

The gals and I had a good time. One of them asked where I was deadheading to.

"Oh, I'm not an airline pilot," I said. "I am the captain of a ship."

One stewardess jumped up and said, "Not an airline pilot?"

"No," I said.

"That will be $14.50, please!" The fun was over.

When we landed at Melbourne, I shook hands with the flight crew and gave each stewardess a New Year's Eve kiss. "Happy New Year!"

Outside the airport terminal, I breathed in the warm air and saw the palms swaying gently in the wind. I was finally home where it was warm, and I could soak up sun on the beach.

The "*Judy*," photo by Bob Campbell

S.S. *JUDITH M. PIERSON*

Ship: *S.S. Judith M. Pierson*
Rank: Captain
Year: 1982

S.S. *Judith M. Pierson* was my next ship to sail for the 1982 season. I really wanted *Soo River Trader* back, but she was not to come out until later in the season. I joined the "*Judy*" in the canal. My first port of call was Hamilton, Ontario, where we were to deliver a load of beans. It often took three days to discharge cargo in Hamilton, so it was a good port for going ashore.

After unloading, we went Thunder Bay and loaded grain for Quebec City. Our trip was uneventful. *Judy* was a very forgiving little ship, and I soon forgot about the *Soo River Trader* and paid all of my attention to my new ship.

121

We were upbound (headed away from the Atlantic) in the South Shore Canal, and I was talking to another of our company's ships, steamer *Joan M. McCullough*, which was downbound in the same waterway. As we rounded the last corner of the canal, I saw the *McCullough* right in the center of the canal headed toward us. Surely, the captain would move over to his side to allow us to meet safely. But he didn't give me an inch of room, and I had to move over toward the bank to keep from colliding with him.

After we passed each other, the stern of the ship started to get sucked toward the bank, and the front of the ship was protruding out into the center of the canal. I thought, "This is where we go aground," but at the last moment, I rang up full astern, hoping the cavitation (air bubbles) from the prop would cause the stern to work itself back into the center of the canal, which it did. *Judy* was a very forgiving ship!

The shipping season went along very smoothly with the *Judy*. One day, while upbound in the St. Marys River, I received a phone call from my office. It was Captain Ron Dean asking my location.

"We're just below Nine Mile Point," I responded.

Captain Dean ordered, "Turn the ship around as soon as you can and proceed directly to Owen Sound. When you get there, lay up the ship and pay off the crew. You can stay aboard as shipkeeper until further orders."

Not really sure what was up, I phoned the chief with the news. He was as bewildered as I was about the situation.

Getting the Bad News

Once we were headed downbound, a small boat came up to our starboard bow. A guy with a camera and recorder shouted, "Hey, Cap! Can you blow me a salute?"

I told the mate to blow this guy a salute with the *Judy's* old steam whistle, and I stepped out of the pilothouse to get my picture taken. "Send me one, will you?" I yelled down to the boat.

He did indeed send me that picture. In fact, he sent me pictures of the entire *Soo River Fleet*. Many years later, I finally met him—his name is Bob Campbell—and we became friends.

When *Judith M. Pierson* arrived at Owen Sound, we found out that the Soo River Company was in receivership. Everyone felt such a sense of loss! After I paid off each crewmember and shook their hands goodbye, I was alone on a dead ship. I would be there for two months.

But life was good shipkeeping on the *Judy*. All that I had to do was pump out the bilge tanks every morning and pull the ladder up to keep inquisitive people from coming aboard. I sat in the sun and tanned all day while receiving full skipper's pay. The only problem was my cooking. It definitely was not like the Twine House!

Too Much to Eat

I had one problem: there was all this food aboard. I could not possibly use it all before it spoiled. I counted over 30 cases of fresh milk, 3 crates of eggs, all kinds of vegetables, frozen meats, and 25 pounds of butter. It was enough food to feed 30 men for a week. I didn't want to waste any of it, so I called a hospital and an old age home, and offered it to them. But no one would take it off my hands because of bureaucratic nonsense. It was perfectly good, fresh food, and nobody wanted it.

That same afternoon, I saw an old couple walking to the A&P store pushing a wheeled cart. I walked up to them, and of course, both eyed me up suspiciously. I told them who I was and why I was there. "Do you want some free food?" I asked. "Bring your friends down to the ship, too, and I'll give you all the food you can carry home."

Before I got back to the ship, there was a line of people a block long: people carrying baskets, pulling wagons and carts, all waiting for me to lower the ladder. I got rid of all the food, leaving just enough for me to live on while I was shipkeeping.

The galley on the Trader; photo by Dick Metz

In the freezer, I had found a huge, well-wrapped pork roast, so I thought I would make myself a pork feast and use the leftovers for pork sandwiches for lunches for days to come. Being the cook that I am, I remembered that when cooking pork, one should make sure to cook it until well-done, leaving none of the meat red or pink. With this in mind, I turned on the oven, put the meat inside, and planned to check on it in about three hours. When it was done, I'd roast my potatoes and have a hearty meal.

I did some chores and came back after three hours. When I peeked at the roast, it was still red, so back into the oven it went. A few hours later, I could smell pork all over the ship. In fact, I figured anyone in the harbor could smell it. So I checked it again, fully expecting it to be golden brown. But it was still red inside, although it had shrunk noticeably. Back into the oven it went.

A little later, a fishing buddy showed up with a catch of lake trout for me, and we walked back to the galley to put the fish into the freezer. While there, I went to the oven and checked the roast again. It had shrunk even smaller, but it was still red inside.

"What do you suppose is wrong with this piece of pork?" I asked my friend. "I've been roasting it for hours and it's still not done."

He took a peek at the meat. "Your trouble is, this is not a pork roast. It is a ham!"

The ham was so tough and salty that I had to feed it to the seagulls.

Painting Over the Name

One day, I heard banging against the hull, so I looked down over the ship's side. There was a man standing there, and he asked me, "Do you have any black paint?"

"Yes, I do," I replied.

"Well, you can paint out the Soo River Company on the ship's side and also the name *Judith M. Pierson*."

"And who might you be, telling me to paint this entirely out?" I yelled down to him.

"Captain Norm Ball, marine superintendent for P&H Shipping Company."

P&H, I had heard the name before, and it did not appeal to me at all.

Like it or not, the next morning I got out the black paint and painted over the white letters that spelled Soo River Company. I painted out the *Judith M. Pierson* name on both bows and on the fantail. Under P&H, her new name was *Fernglen*.

I was shipkeeper on the *Judy/Fernglen* in Owen Sound for eight weeks. Then a crew was sent aboard and I received orders to load at the Great Lakes elevator in Owen Sound for delivery to Montreal. When we departed Owen Sound's harbor, I looked back over the stern at the little city that was growing smaller by the minute. Everyone had been so nice to me there; I was going to miss it.

On our return trip upbound, my phone rang. The mate said, "Gale warnings are up on Superior, Cap!"

Headed up the St. Marys River for the MacArthur Lock, we passed the museum ship *Valley Camp*, a sister ship to the *Judy/Fernglen*. "Here we go again with gales," I thought. "And here I am going out into storm-tossed Lake Superior with *Fernglen*, and her sister ship is a museum!" But even as *Fernglen*, the forgiving little ship lived up to her reputation.

We laid up in Toronto that winter, and I was the last captain to sail the Fernglen. She stayed there tied up alongside *Pineglen*, and a few years later, both ships went to the scrapyard.

After P&H bought out the bankrupt Soo River Company, they scrapped their smaller ships, such as *Birchglen*, *Cedarglen*, *Fernglen*, *Pineglen* and *Elmglen*, replacing them with *Oakglen*, *Willowglen*, *Beechglen* and *Mapleglen*. Reducing the fleet meant that master's jobs were scarce. At first, I became a relief captain, and then I went back to serving as first mate for a while.

The first ship named *Oakglen*; photo by Bob Campbell

BEATING THE STORM

○○○○○○○○○○○○○○○○○

Ship: *Oakglen (1)*
Rank: Oakglen
Year: 1923

○○○○○○○○○○○○○○○○○

On November 22, 1983, I was master of the old *Oakglen*—it was built in 1953—and we departed the MacArthur Lock at the Soo Locks for a load of grain at Thunder Bay, Ontario.

As the ship's stern cleared the lock gates headed for Lake Superior, I took a look at the latest weather via the MAFOR—a marine forecast in numerical code—for the big lake. Northeast gales were predicted in about 18 hours. I figured the old girl would have enough time to waddle her way across the lake to Passage Island before the blow hit. Normally, I would choose to go up along the North Shore in a Nor'easter. But since we had plenty of time and the wind and sea were calm all the way out past Whitefish Point, I gave orders to take the regular course of 300 degrees for Passage Island, which is north of Isle Royale. Once inside of Passage, we would have a good ride to Thunder Bay. So we went up the center of the lake, and all went well for the first half of the crossing.

About nine hours out, I was in my quarters and I noticed that the ship engine had stopped vibrating. My ship's service phone rang. "Engine trouble," said the mate on watch. I hurried up the stairs to the bridge.

"Cap, we've lost one cylinder on the main engine," came the diagnosis from Chief Engineer Ralph Morris, who had called from the engine room.

I put on my hat and coat and walked down the deck back to the engine room to confer with the chief. The wind was freshening from the northeast.

The cylinder was indeed damaged; I could see that. "About the only thing I can do," said Ralph, "is to isolate that cylinder. That means we'll chug the rest of the way to Thunder Bay at less than half speed."

"Okay, Chief, you're the boss. How long do you figure it will take to isolate the cylinder and get underway again?" I casually mentioned the approaching gale due to reach us in nine hours or so.

"Give me four hours, Cap," the Chief answered.

Our time was running out with the gale, but I didn't have any choice but to let him do what needed to be done.

"Okay, Chief, give it your best shot. Remember, we're floating around the middle of the lake with that gale bearing down on us."

Making Repairs

The chief barked orders to his men; they lost no time working with their hammers and the chain hoist. I left the chief alone with his crew to perform their dirty job and headed back forward. As I walked up the deck, I estimated the wind was blowing about 15 knots. "I hope that Nor'easter is not on time," I thought. "I need a few more hours." But that was wishful thinking, that's all it was.

The four hours the chief promised came and went. The wind was increasing every hour. I didn't want to call the chief to ask how they were doing; I knew that he and his engine room crew were doing their best on that cylinder, and he didn't need the interruption.

A radio broadcast from the Sault Ste. Marie Coast Guard changed my mind. The forecast was now for gales becoming storms on Lake Superior. I walked back to the engine room again to find out how much longer.

In the engine room, chains had been tied around the cylinder, and it was hoisted up and away from the crankshaft. Being powerless, the *Oakglen* was broadside to the wind and sea and had started a lazy roll. No one had to be told that the gale was coming closer.

Alone with the chief, I said, "Ralph, make sure you secure that cylinder so when we start to roll and the cylinder starts swinging back and forth, the chains won't snap and let the cylinder fall into the turning crank. That would be game over."

"Yes, sir, and we will be ready to get out of here in one more hour." The chief walked off.

Another hour was lost that I did not want to lose.

Getting Underway

I was waiting in the wheelhouse about an hour later, when the chief called.

"We're ready to go."

A steam turbine; photo by Dick Metz

I rang up full ahead and put her back on the 300-degree heading, and we were underway, but full ahead was now only six knots, just under seven miles per hour. We crawled our way up the lake for Passage Island.

About three hours from Passage and in the lee of the land (where the land protected us from the wind), the ship started to roll pretty good. The Nor'easter had freshened even more.

An hour later, a call from the galley announced that the freezer had fallen over in front of the reefer door, and the porter and second cook were trapped inside. The steward and others back aft were working to free them.

By this time, the ship had more than a moderate roll. It was time to smooth out the ride. "Hard to port!" I ordered. " As her stern came around into the sea, the old girl settled right down with a following sea. It wasn't a direct route, but it was safer.

The women got out of the reefer unharmed, except for me. Glenna, the second cook, scolded me for rolling the ship. And everybody listened to Glenna!

When we were only 15 miles from Passage Island, I hauled her around for Rock of Ages Lighthouse. *Oakglen* was riding well in the following sea, and the wind was consistently gale force as we headed for the "Rock." Most of the crew could now settle down for a well-deserved rest, but not me. I had to figure out my plan for rounding Rock of Ages Light at the southwestern tip of Isle Royale. At that point, I would be exposing the ship's side to the wind and sea during the turn around the lighthouse and onto the new course for Angus Island and the entrance to Thunder Bay.

My experience working on Isle Royale paid off for me now. I remembered a fisherman once told me that a calm will accrue two miles southwest of Rock of Ages. It had something to do with the topography of the lake bottom and nearby reefs, so I set course for two miles off the light to see if the old fisherman was right.

As we neared the turn around the lighthouse, I had the mate call all departments, telling them to make sure everything aboard was secured down tightly. "When you hear the whistle blow, hang on."

"How's our suspended cylinder?" I asked the chief.

"Okay, Cap."

As we came up to the light, I looked ahead with my field glasses for a kind of a calm, not really expecting to see any change in this sea that had done nothing but increase over the past few hours. "Behold, the eye of the viewer." The old fisherman knew what he was talking about. There was just such a spot where the waves weren't as high.

One long blast on the ship's whistle, and when the timing was just right, I ordered the wheel starboard and to keep the light abeam (parallel to the ship) all the way around to our new course that would take us to Angus Island. *Oakglen* came around very nicely to the new heading. Everything was okay, at least for now.

A Gale Turns into a Storm

We were sailing northeast between Isle Royale and the Minnesota shoreline when the full fury of the gale turned to a storm. We had some shelter offered by Isle Royale, however, and the ship was riding well. Closer to Angus Island, we would again be exposed to a mean Nor'easter. I had some time before that, so I went back to the engine room to check on the damaged cylinder.

She was wrapped up like a lady in a tight dress and there was a timber lying across the gap into the engine, so if she would break loose, she would not fall into the crankshaft and disable the ship. The engine room gang had done a good job in securing everything. Satisfied, I returned to the pilothouse to think about my next move in trying to outsmart Mother Nature.

Into the Storm

When we were parallel to Angus Island, we met the full brunt of the storm. The mate clocked the wind at a steady 65 mph with gusts from 70 to 75 mph. I knew that we could not make the turn around Angus Island without going broadside to the sea and exposing the entire length of the ship to the wind.

Captain Rick Hulst aboard the steamer *Birchglen* over at Thunder Bay called to say that the seas were washing over the breakwalls and all tug service was suspended until the storm died out. I decided I wouldn't try going through the piers. Instead, I headed for Thunder Cape. Once behind the cape, we would be in calmer water where we could anchor. Inside the cape, I turned for a suitable spot, got into position, and ordered the anchor dropped. After the hook was down, I backed her slow in order for the anchor to dig in and hold. She seemed to be holding, so I warned the mate to check her position to make sure she did not drag the anchor, and I went to my quarters.

The Oakglen's bridge

I was about to lie down in bed, which looked very inviting to me. "The hook's not holding," came the mate's voice on the phone. "The wind's blowing us off position." Up to the bridge I went again.

We pulled the anchor up and moved to a different spot and dropped it again and waited. I didn't go down to my bed this time. After 20 minutes, the mate took another position. "She's slipping again." We were facing a wind that was blowing over the top of Thunder Cape and all the way down the side, gathering speed down the mountain and then blowing out over the water, right into us.

At this point, I felt that I had just enough stuff in me to do it one more time, which we did. This time the anchor held. After being up on the bridge for 38 hours, I went to bed.

The anchor held fast all night. The next morning the wind began to diminish, so we raised the anchor again and turned around. We headed for Thunder Bay shipyard to get our engine repaired, which took several days. We left the shipyard and loaded our cargo of grain at Cargill elevator and left for the Seaway.

The *Soo River Trader*; photo by Tom Salver

MAKE LOVE TO THAT NORTH SHORE

Ship: *Soo River Trader*
Rank: Captain
Year: 1983

We departed the Soo Locks and headed for Thunder Bay with east gales blowing. I remembered what old Captain Bill Smith had once told me about traveling in bad weather, "Make love to that North Shore; she will be your friend." With this in mind, I headed the bow of the old ship up the North Shore of Lake Superior.

Once on top of the big lake, I planned to haul around and set course for Thunder Bay.

At the same time, the wind was predicted to shift back to the northeast and then again to the north. Sometimes, the weatherman is way off in his prediction. This was one of those times. The eastern gale turned into an easterly storm and would stay that way for at least 18 hours.

We reduced speed to half ahead, as we were in no hurry to get to the top of the lake. We sailed up on the inside of Michipicoten Island, and the sea was picking up. We could hear the wind whistling through the wheelhouse doors and windows, as it must have done for over 76 years on the old *Soo River Trader*.

A 1000-footer was right behind us on the way to Duluth. Even that huge ship had to stay in the lee of the Ontario land for protection from the wind.

A few hours later, and still going half speed, we were nearing the top end of the lake, and I knew there was no way that I was going across to Thunder Bay in an easterly storm. Although I would have the wind and sea to my back all the way across Superior, when I reached Battle Island Light, I would have to turn and expose my port (left) side to the elements.

What if we had an engine failure? No, sir! It was too many "ifs" for me. I decided we would stay put where we were, and we would have a comfortable ride out of it.

Soon our easy ride was in jeopardy. The wind was really howling, and we were getting a backwash from shore. As we didn't have cargo and only had ballast aboard, we were rolling pretty good. I talked to the captain of the 1000-footer, who was still behind me, and he reported that he was also rolling.

The situation had deteriorated to the point that I did not like the spot we were in, so I got out the harbor charts for the east side of the lake.

I looked at Marathon, Ontario, and the possibility of anchoring in the bay there until the storm blew itself out. A few years before, I had taken *D. C. Everest* out of that harbor and headed for Thunder Bay, so I knew the area somewhat. After a close study of the chart, I made up my mind that we would go into Marathon Harbor and ride the anchor. My first mate, Peter Columbus, drew the course lines on the chart for entering the harbor. I checked the courses, and decided that was the best course of action to take.

"We're going to anchor in Marathon Harbor," I told the 1000-footer captain.

He replied, "I wish we were smaller, because I would follow right in behind you. Good luck, Cap!"

When we turned to make the harbor entrance, I could make out the large mountains on both sides of the entry. While looking from one side to the other through the field glasses,

Never what you want to see

I saw white shoal water just ahead of me! Terrified, I told Peter what I saw. He looked through his glasses and confirmed what I had seen.

I ran to the radar. I rechecked our position. I ran to the table to recheck the chart. We were certainly in the right position to make the entrance to the harbor. What was that white water?

We were too close inside to stop or back her up, so we had no choice but to continue. I had the feeling that I was right and I was wrong—all at the same time. But we kept going. The white water grew nearer and nearer. We were close enough that I could see the lights of buildings inside the harbor. My hands were sweaty. I felt little beads of saltwater running down my backbone.

Peter yelled, "Cap, it's foam!"

"What?" I looked through my glasses again, and now I could see a ridge of thick, white foam. It was being held across the entrance by the east wind and current coming back into the harbor.

The office aboard the Soo River Trader

What a relief! But I lost some of my hair that night.

Safely inside, we picked out a good, deep spot and let go the anchor. Even inside the harbor, the ship was still rolling lazily. We rolled all that night and half of the next day before we could finally pick up our anchor and head for Thunder Bay. The 1000-footer was moving, too.

I sailed *Soo River Trader* for the rest of that season and laid her up in Toronto, never to sail the old girl again.

She was my favorite ship.

The *Soo River Trader* at the Scrapper

Two years later, I made a trip to Port Maitland, Ontario, to watch the scrapper's torch cut my favorite ship into two-foot-square blocks.

"Who are you and what are you doing here?" the foreman asked me.

"This was my favorite ship," I told him. "Two years ago, I was captain of her."

"Well, okay, Cap, go aboard, and if you find anything you want to take home for a souvenir, you can have it. Take your time."

I walked around the gaps where pieces of steel had already been cut away and made my way into the dining room, where Glenna served me many fine meals. I found a salt shaker standing alone inside a bulkhead. I reached over, picked it up, and stuck it into my pocket.

Then I worked my way forward and up to the bridge where I went to the front window and stared out. I remembered the storm-tossed night that I brought her into Marathon Harbor, and the white "shoal" water that, for a moment, threatened to ground the ship.

The *Willowglen*; photo by Marc Dease

BECOMING A *WILLOWGLEN*-ER

Ship: *Willowglen*
Rank: Captain
Year: 1993

At the beginning of World War II, the US Maritime Commission ordered the construction of 16 ships for the Great Lakes fleet; these were built to support the war effort and to ensure that enough iron ore could be transported from the mines to the steel mills. To that end, the ships were designed to be larger and have more carrying capacity than anything on the lakes at the time.

Since the Maritime Commission ordered the 16 vessels, they soon became known as Maritime Class vessels, or "Maritimers," a nickname that has stuck with them ever since. The Commission named them after the various iron ore ranges scattered across the

Upper Midwest. The 16 sister ships were all 620 feet long, with a 60-foot beam (beam is a vessel's width at the widest point), a depth of 35 feet, and a carrying capacity in excess of 18,000 tons.

The first of these vessels to be delivered was the *Thomas Wilson*, and the last Maritimer built was the *Mesabi*. I sailed on both of them. My first deckhand job was on the *Wilson*, and I was the last captain to sail the *Mesabi*, the sixteenth Maritimer, after she had been sold to P&H Shipping Company and renamed *Willowglen*.

Built as the *Mesabi*, the ship that would become the *Willowglen* was first renamed *Lehigh* and delivered to Bethlehem Steel Corporation in 1943. She became the first Maritimer to sail under a foreign flag when she was sold to the Canadian Soo River Company in 1981 and was renamed *Joseph X. Robert*. (On the Great Lakes, ships sometimes go through quite a few names.)

In 1982, she was sold again, to P&H Shipping Company and renamed *Willowglen*.

Trouble started right away for *Willowglen*. She was plagued with engine trouble and then boiler problems. She was getting old and was underpowered for the long runs down the Seaway. Quite often, she was at anchor or tied to a dock, awaiting repairs.

Her "claim to fame" came as she was headed upbound (away from the Atlantic) at Port Huron just below the Blue Water Bridge. The current caught her starboard bow, and without enough power to fight the current, she slammed head-on into the concrete wall below the bridge. For a long time afterward, a large chunk was missing from the spot where she hit.

When the captain's wife took ill and he had to go home, I was transferred over from the *Mapleglen*—which was the company's flagship at the time—to the *Willowglen*.

I joined the *Willowglen* in Owen Sound, Ontario. "What a ratty ship compared to the *Mapleglen*," I thought. Of course, the crew told me that I was not a *Willowglen*-er, and they were right.

The *Willowglen*; photo by Marc Dease

We made several trips down the Seaway with grain, and the old girl handled pretty well. But when fully loaded down with heavy iron ore in her belly and going upstream in the St. Lawrence, she became a nightmare to handle.

With only 2500 horsepower, the *Willowglen* was under-powered. Her old steam steering gear, which helped turn the rudder, was worn out. She should have been retired, but that was not the case.

On *Willowglen's* final trip upbound from Quebec City to Burns Harbor, Indiana, we were approaching the Snell Lock. Once under the Seaway International Bridge, I encountered so much current that the wheelsman had to steer all the way over with the wheel one way, then back the other way to keep her heading straight for the tie-up wall below the Snell. Her head would take off to port (left) while the wheelsman applied a hard starboard rudder and hoped that she would eventually come back to the center of the river.

It worked. We made it to the Welland Canal without a mishap, but that would change. After departing one of the locks, the steam steering gear started acting up. I had the watchman stand by the anchors just in case we lost our steering. We made seven of the eight locks without any trouble, but my hair was getting thinner.

I got the green light to enter Lock 8. "The last one," I thought, "and we'll be home free."

"Watch the set to port (make sure the ship doesn't head to the left)," I warned the wheelsman as we came up to the Robin Hood Flour Mill. A small river emptied into the canal there, causing a strong current.

I looked up at the rudder indicator, and it was showing the ship turning to the left.

"Hard to starboard!" I yelled. It was too late. The current caught the bow, and the ship came up hard on the wall. The lockmaster saw what had happened, and the Seaway made sure the ship was inspected before we departed Lock 8. Except for a dented plate, the old girl did not hurt herself. Despite her shortcomings, she was built like a tank! (They built steel ships back in those days.) Then we were out of the canal, and there was no more stopping until Burns Harbor, Indiana, where our cargo would be unloaded. The ship struggled as she carried this heavy load of iron ore for so many hundreds of miles.

Fueling Up

It was time to think about fuel. I called the P&H office to ask what our next load was to be. On our upbound trips, we usually stopped for fuel at Shell Oil in Sarnia, Ontario. I didn't want to stop at Sarnia for fuel this time if I didn't have to, because the fuel dock was located too close to the Blue Water Bridge. *Willowglen*, as I had discovered, was underpowered and slow, especially when loaded. If I tried to stop at the Blue Water Bridge, I wouldn't have enough distance to gain enough speed to make the turn.

"Nothing to worry about," was the answer that came over the phone. "You will be going to Toledo for grain, then on to Port Colborne to discharge and at the same time, refuel."

Golden words! Now I had a good shot at full speed for that dreaded bridge.

I told my chief engineer, Murray Patterson, "I want all the steam you can coax out of the old boilers, because I need it to make my run for the bridge."

He assured me, "I'll squeeze out every last pound of steam. We'll even shut off all the steam to the crew quarters. Just let me know when we are safely past the bridge, so I can back off on the steam."

"Okay," I said. "Chief, thank you."

As we approached the bridge, I checked the wind direction, hoping it was not blowing out of the north, which would make the turn even harder. But the Lake Huron gods were on my side. Light winds were from the south.

I turned to the wheelsman. "Listen very carefully to my steering commands. Under no circumstances let the ship fall off to the port side."

"Yes, sir, Cap," he said.

We had a few guests aboard on that trip, and all the talk was about how the ship had not made the turn on the last trip and had crashed into the wall at Port Huron. I didn't want a repeat of that occurrence.

As we closed in for the bridge, I called up the Chief. "Okay, Murray, give me everything the old girl has left." I rang up double full ahead on the Engine Order Telegram.

Thick, black smoke billowed from the stack, as all the steam we had was fed to the old girl's engine. I noticed that all of my guests were standing in the wheelhouse. Bill Parker, our second mate, had his wife, Irene, aboard for the trip, and they hadn't spent much time in the wheelhouse. But they were there now. Everyone was watching. I had my eye glued to the front of the bow, anticipating even the tiniest movement to port before the ship entered the main region of the heavy river current.

"Hard to starboard," I ordered, "and try to keep it hard over till I tell you different." The rudder indicator went hard over, and the ship was steady, or was she? No! The bow was going off to port! All I could imagine was another hole in that concrete wall, right next to the last one. I kept on saying to myself, "Come on, baby, move back to starboard."

It seemed like an eternity to me before I noticed that she stopped turning to port. Would she? Come on, old girl, be good to Daddy; come to starboard for me.

The Willowglen under tow; photo by James Hoffman

146

At last, the bow started to creep to starboard and to the center of the bridge. The old girl went right up under the bridge and out into the calm waters of Lake Huron. I called the chief, "You can cut her back down now. Thanks again." The chief engineer on any ship is worth his weight in gold, and Murray was just that chief.

We turned north through the center of the buoys, and someone said, "Nice job, Cap."

I replied, "Piece of cake," as my wobbling legs carried me down to my quarters. I had just lost five years of my life making that turn.

Losing the Engine

Later, we received orders to proceed to Port Stanley, Ontario, to load grain for Buffalo. We had four trips back-to-back hauling grain to Buffalo. We were traveling at a slow speed about three miles off Port Stanley when we lost our engine.

It was a beautiful, calm day, so I coasted in a wide circle to slow us down. Then I dropped the anchor until the necessary repairs could be made. This was the first of many troubles that would plague *Willowglen* for the rest of the season.

Once the ship was repaired, we had to turn the ship and back in from the piers. It took two days to load at Port Stanley, but no one cared too much because there was a sandy swimming beach next to the ship. (Port Stanley is a great little fishing village with friendly people.)

When we arrived at Buffalo on our first trip, a southwest gale was blowing. The tug office told us we would have to anchor in the harbor and wait for the wind to die down before they would take us and tow us to the elevator up the river. So we anchored.

The next day, two tugs hooked up with us and towed the ship up the river to the elevator. There were several tight, 90-degree turns we had to make; on one, the bow just cleared the concrete abutment of a bridge with only two feet to spare.

Since unloading would take a day or so, I took the opportunity to explore the city of Buffalo. I liked Buffalo right from the start. Small shops and secondhand stores lined both sides of the wide streets. At night, Buffalo is a beautiful city with all the lights surrounding the harbor.

On those trips to Buffalo, I had the pleasure of walking out to Buffalo's Naval and Military Park, where I ate one of the city's famous hot dogs, which I washed down with a cold beer. There, I went aboard the submarine USS *Croaker* and the

The USS *Croaker* at Buffalo's Naval and Military Park

USS *Sullivan Brothers*, which are both tied up in the harbor as tourist attractions.

The Race

On another trip, another captain was aboard—Captain Stanley—as I was training him on the *Willowglen*. *Beechglen* was behind us as we departed the Soo Locks upbound for Thunder Bay. The *Beech*, being the faster of the two ships, quickly took the lead and headed out across Lake Superior.

Captain Larry Leveille was in command of *Beechglen*. As both ships raced across eastern Lake Superior, southwest gale warnings went up for all of the big lake.

Larry called and said, "We're going to favor the South Shore." This route would allow him to take advantage of the lee of the land (the part of the land out of the wind), which provided calmer waters.

I talked the situation over with Captain Stanley, and we agreed to follow the South Shore as well. By now, *Beechglen* was miles ahead of us.

As the hours passed, the wind began howling and the sea picked up strength every hour. *Willowglen* was a better sea boat than the *Beech*. With this in mind, we headed for Keweenaw Point with the possibility of anchoring in Bete Grise Bay to wait out the storm.

By this time, the *Beechglen* was already waiting out the weather in Keweenaw Bay. When Larry heard about our plan, he also headed for Bete Grise, although he did not relish the idea of being hidden way down in Keweenaw Bay and the *Willowglen* miles ahead of him.

When we arrived off Keweenaw Point, I called a down-bound freighter off Copper Harbor.

"How are you doing out there?"

"We're riding the seas very well," he reported.

Stan and I agreed to go around the point and head for Rock of Ages Light to bring the bow of the ship into the wind and sea. *Willowglen* rode very well.

We called Larry. "We rounded the point," I told him, "and we're riding well into the head sea." (This means with the bow heading into the wind and seas.)

In the background, we could hear Larry yelling something like, "Those two bastards are going to kill themselves!" But Larry could not bear the thought of us being ahead of him, so around the point he came.

The *Beechglen* passed us again. She was a mile ahead and heading for Devils Island when we altered course for the Rock of Ages Lighthouse. We were still having a good ride out of it. So we called Larry again. "How are you doing?" I asked.

The mate said, "Well, we're riding pretty rough."

We could hear Larry in the background again. "I should have stayed at anchor behind the point instead of following those two bastards out here."

I turned to Stan. "Years ago, fishermen told me about a calm (an area known for being calm) just southwest of the Rock of Ages Lighthouse. It worked for me on the *Oakglen* once. What do you think?"

We agreed to try it again with the *Willowglen*. And it worked again. We came around the Rock two miles off and steered for Angus Island.

Larry was flabbergasted when he heard we turned at the Rock. We were ahead of him again.

He was many miles off to the southwest and still cussing us out. By the time we got to Angus Island, the *Beechglen* passed us once more heading for Thunder Bay.

I thought about telling Stan that I knew a shortcut to Thunder Bay by going behind Pie Island, which would put us ahead of Larry one more time and we would arrive at Thunder Bay first. I knew Stan would go for it. But after I thought about Larry and all the bad times we had given him on this trip, I decided not to mention the shortcut to Stan. Larry would never have forgiven me if we had arrived in Thunder Bay ahead of him.

Upgrades

In the fall of 1992, we put *Willowglen* into Port Weller Dry Docks for her five-year inspection—each ship gets inspected for seaworthiness every five years. While she was sitting high and dry on the blocks, I walked under the hull of the ship. What a sensation it was! There I stood with thousands of tons above me. I noticed how sound the hull looked; there weren't many dents in the plating.

P&H had the shipyard install a new propeller on the old shaft. Ten days later, we were all inspected and ready to go. I had high hopes for the old girl with a new prop and a new steering gear installed. Nothing could go wrong now, or so I thought.

We headed for Toledo for a load of grain to be delivered to Montreal. While loading in Toledo, the wind blew from the west. It blew stronger and stronger, and blew much of the water out of the Maumee River. As the port was based in the Maumee River, we sat there for a few days.

A Close Call

When the water came back in and we finished loading, the wind again began blowing from the west. I called the tug office. "I want to leave now, before the water goes out again," I told the dispatcher.

Soon we handed our bow line to the tug and cut the *Willowglen* loose. The tug pulled ahead in an attempt to get our bow to clear some wooden pilings that were coming up to the ship fast. The current had gotten hold of the ship. I was backing full astern (reverse) with the aid of a tug, and the pilings just kept getting closer and closer. "Give her everything you've got!" I yelled to the tug skipper.

"The bow's going to come up on the pilings," I thought, and I was still going full astern. I imagined how this would sit with the company with the ship just leaving the shipyard yesterday.

The watchman had run up to the bow. He turned and yelled up to me at the front window, "We're clear by inches!"

I lost more hair again that day.

The Last Trip

Willowglen made several uneventful trips down the St. Lawrence Seaway. Our last trip that season was into Goderich,

Ontario, to unload, and over to Owen Sound, Ontario, on Georgian Bay for layup. *Willowglen* had her ride through a gale when we departed Goderich. Northwest gales were up again on Lake Huron when we were ready to leave. Meanwhile, *Mapleglen* had arrived in Goderich to unload, making the small harbor a bit tight for me to get around and out.

Nevertheless, we steamed out of Goderich harbor at full speed and steered for the Michigan shoreline to pick up some shelter and make a good ride out of it, this being our last trip of the season. We arrived in Owen Sound and laid up *Willowglen*, not knowing that this would be her last trip forever.

The End of the *Willowglen*

As it happens, she wouldn't sail again. *Willowglen* remained in Owen Sound for several years. Then she was returned to Goderich as a grain storage barge. The old girl still sits there today with her shiny new propeller sticking out of the water, never to turn again.

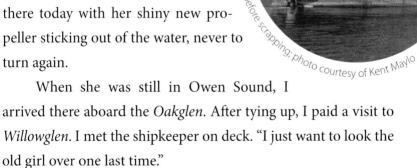

The *Willowglen* before scrapping; photo courtesy of Kent Maylo

When she was still in Owen Sound, I arrived there aboard the *Oakglen*. After tying up, I paid a visit to *Willowglen*. I met the shipkeeper on deck. "I just want to look the old girl over one last time."

This was fine with him, as he wanted to go downtown for a few supplies. When he was in town, I salvaged the two brass mast-head lights and both sidelights. Today I have the two sidelights mounted in my home, and the two masthead lights mounted as my garage lights. I look at them every now and then and try to imagine how many storms that they must have gone through. I also fondly remember the time that we raced Larry across Lake Superior.

The *Oakglen*; photo courtesy of www.boatnerd.com

RELIEF CAPTAIN

Ship: *Oakglen* and *Mapleglen*
Rank: Captain
Year: Throughout the 1990s

In the mid and late 1990s, P&H Shipping Company had two ships in service, *Oakglen* and *Mapleglen*. I was relief captain for the two ships, filling in when other captains weren't available.

I enjoyed the role of relief captain, since I missed fit out and the early part of the season, as well as most of the late fall storms that frequented the lakes. I usually missed out on the layup of the ships, too. I just sailed during the warm summer months while the other two captains took their vacations.

The men who crewed these ships were all professional sailors with many years sailing on the same ship. One such professional was wheelsman Kenny Budgel, who was wheeling on the *Oakglen* for one of my 35-day sailing periods.

The company called me at home in Florida, and I was to report aboard *Oakglen* the next day. I spent a day flying and sitting around in airport lobbies. Then I had a four-hour drive to Owen Sound to join the ship.

When I arrived, I was already beat, but I stayed up until we were unloaded, and we then departed for Thunder Bay. Thinking that I would catch up on some sleep while underway, I went to bed. But I could not fall asleep until we departed the Soo Locks.

I had fallen into a really sound sleep and did not notice that the ship was starting to take on a lazy roll, which increased as the hours passed. Third Mate George Parsons woke me up. "Cap, I think we should alter course," he said.

When I came fully awake, she was rolling pretty well. In fact, I couldn't believe what I saw. All my furniture and books were strewn around the room. I had a difficult time just walking to the wheelhouse stairs. When I finally got to the foot of the stairs, I yelled up to Kenny, "Hard to port and come around to 240 degrees!"

Kenny, being the pro that he was, repeated my order and brought her around to have the sea on our stern. The ship rode a lot better that way.

The wheelhouse was also a mess. Charts and chairs were lying all over the place. I couldn't believe that the rolling had not woken me up. That night at dinner, I received a mean glare from our Chief Cook, Glenna. "Cap, you never rolled a ship like this for so long before."

What could I say? That I was sleeping? Glenna had me nailed, and she knew it!

Traveling on the Keweenaw on the *Mapleglen*

The Keweenaw Waterway is about 25 miles long, cutting the northern part of Michigan's Upper Peninsula in half; the two sections of the Keweenaw Peninsula are bridged only by the Houghton-Hancock Bridge. In summer and fall, the hillsides along the waterway were beautiful, especially when the leaves changed color. I had been through the waterway many times with the National Park Service tug years before, and I always enjoyed the trip as far as Houghton. I was looking for an excuse to transit the waterway with a big ship.

My transit finally happened in the fall of 1996 while I was on the *Mapleglen*. We departed the Soo Locks bound for Superior, Wisconsin. We were parallel to Whitefish Point, and southwest

The *Mapleglen*; photo by Todd Davidson

storm warnings were posted for all of Lake Superior. The mate and I studied the charts to figure out a course that would result in a good, safe ride across the lake.

I thought that southwest winds would be ideal for the waterway, so we set course for the lower entrance of the Keweenaw Waterway. By the next day, the storm raged with winds up to 70 knots (about 80 miles per hour) off Stannard Rock Lighthouse. We entered Keweenaw Bay, but the storm was blowing with thick snow and too much wind to try for the entrance. We anchored in Pequaming Bay until the next day. I really wanted to make the trip through the waterway in the fall to see the colors. I knew this would be my only chance, and I intended to take it.

The next day, we entered the breakwall leading into the waterway. Snow was still falling. My trusted first mate, George Power, was on the radar with me at the front window as we headed through the Portage River. We slowly steamed ahead. At times, the snow fell so thickly that it was a total whiteout. It was an interesting trip; we passed small fishing villages and 100-year-old abandoned homes.

The winds were predicted to veer to the west while remaining at storm strength, so I told the boys that we would anchor again in Portage Lake, in the middle of the Keweenaw Waterway, and wait for the wind to blow itself out. Before attempting to navigate the canal on the other side of the lake that would take us back out into Lake Superior, we had to make sure the ship would clear the Houghton-Hancock Lift Bridge. We calculated that the aft mast (the mast toward the rear of the ship) would clear the underside of the bridge by a good four feet.

A Tight Fit

While at anchor, I remeasured and calculated everything again, and once again determined that she would clear the lift bridge. I called the bridge tender to see if everything was in order with the bridge and that it'd be operating when we were ready to start moving again.

"We're all set to go," he assured me. "Just give me your ETA when you're underway."

The next morning, the wind was dying down, so we got the engine warmed up. I called the bridge to say we were under-way and gave him our ETA. The snow had let up, so everybody was out on deck to watch the scenery, as many of our Canadian crew had never been through the waterway before.

The Houghton-Hancock Bridge today

When we came around the last bend of the river and saw the bridge ahead, I thought out loud. "What is wrong with that bridge? Look how low to the water it is."

I called the tender. "Why isn't the bridge raised higher? Is something wrong?"

"That's as high as she goes, Cap," was his answer.

We got closer and it looked more and more like we were not going to pass safely under it. "We're not going to make it," said one of the mates.

The chief phoned from back aft. "She's not going to clear the bridge."

For a moment I wished we had not come this way. But I trusted the math and proceeded slowly.

Under the bridge we went, with four feet to spare.

The bridge tender waved. I blew him a salute; he returned the salute from the bridge's horn.

The last time I had been through the waterway was on a 45-foot tugboat and there was lots of room on the waterway. Things were different on a 715-foot freighter. It was a pretty tight fit in some places, and there were several hairpin turns. But we got to the upper entrance without incident, and out into angry Lake Superior we went. I had finally made my trip through the entire Keweenaw Waterway.

A Christmas Trip

I was all finished with my tour of duty for the 1996 season and was planning on spending Christmas at home with my family. Then the office called to ask if I would come back up for one last trip, since the *Oakglen's* regular captain was hospitalized in Owen Sound with heart troubles.

Well, I couldn't refuse, because I knew the crew also wanted to make it home for Christmas. I agreed to fly back up to join the ship in Owen Sound. After all, it was only December 20. The trip to Thunder Bay and back to Owen Sound would only take a few days, and we could all celebrate Christmas at home.

When I got aboard *Oakglen*, the chief had the engine all warmed up and ready to go. We turned in the harbor and headed out through the breakwall into Georgian Bay. We had a nice run up to the Soo and across Lake Superior.

"Piece of cake," I thought as we tied up to Pool #1 in Thunder Bay. I figured we would be loaded and out later that night and back to Owen Sound in plenty of time to make it home for the holidays.

Then I received the afternoon MAFOR (Marine Forecast), and southwest gale warnings were up for all of Lake Superior. We finished loading and departed Thunder Bay for the last time that year.

Inside the Oakglen; photo by Dick Metz

My plan was to run down past Rock of Ages Lighthouse far enough for me to get the wind somewhat on my stern. Meanwhile, the wind increased to storm strength, so I decided to wait it out behind Pie Island where we dropped the anchor.

Celebrating on the Water

Winter storms do not diminish as quickly as summer storms on the big lake. They can blow for several days before dying down. Just because we wanted to get home, I knew it would be one of those long storms. And sure enough, there went our chance for a Christmas at home. We would spend it aboard ship.

At the same time, Captain Richard Samson of *Mapleglen* was upbound ready to take on the ship's last load on at Thunder Bay. Because of the storm, he went to anchor in Bete Grise Bay. Both ships lay at anchor at opposite sides of the lake waiting for weather. We conversed with each other and checked on the wind conditions by radio.

I left word on the bridge to watch the smoke coming out of a large power plant stack in Thunder Bay. When the smoke started to blow from the west, we would try to make the crossing to Copper Harbor. A west wind would be on our stern and afford a comfortable ride across the lake.

Finally, the wind began blowing from the west. We waited a few more hours in order to give the lake time to die down before crossing.

That evening, I decided to give it a try, so up came the hook and we departed for the Rock. Parallel to Rock of Ages Light, I hauled her around for a course that would bring us off Copper Harbor. When we came to our course, it seemed that she was going to ride pretty good.

The helm on the Oakglen; photo by Dick Metz

No Break in the Weather

As luck would have it, though, a strong southwest sea was still left over from the storm, and we were rolling pretty good. So I turned around and went back to anchor behind Pie Island. The wind was still out of the west the next day, so I tried it again. This time the sea had died down enough to make a good ride out of it.

As the cold wind blew down from the north and over the warmer Lake Superior waters, sea smoke started to form in swirling columns of thick fog over the water. It was an eerie sight, like something from another planet.

I called the *Mapleglen* and told Richard, "We're underway, and she's riding good."

"We're underway, too, and riding good," he said.

I figured we would meet each other at mid-lake, so I left word to call me when *Mapleglen* was picked up on radar, and I went below.

I got the call when the *Mapleglen* was close. Because of the Arctic sea smoke, we passed about a half-mile apart without seeing one another.

I called *Mapleglen* and third mate Norman McKay answered. "Merry Christmas to you, the captain, and the crew, from *Oakglen*," I said.

"Yah, okay, Cap," was Norm's answer.

It was December 25, 1999. The crews of both boats were down in the dumps because they did not make it home in time for Christmas.

The galley department, however, prepared the *Oakglen's* crew a wonderful Christmas dinner of roast duck, prime rib, and all the goodies that go along with it. I posted a note on the board that any man who wished to call his family to wish them a Merry Christmas could use my phone to make the call and talk for as long as he liked. Every man called home, and the atmosphere aboard the *Oakglen* improved on that Christmas Day.

The *Beechglen* loading in Buffalo; photo by James Hoffman

FULL ASTERN

○-○-○-○-○-○-○-○-○-○-○-○-○-○-○-○

Ship: *Beechglen*
Rank: Captain
Year: 1991

○-○-○-○-○-○-○-○-○-○-○-○-○-○-○-○

In 1991, I was Master of the *Beechglen* (formerly known as *Pierson Daughters* and originally the *Charles M. Schwab*). As the *Schwab*, her original stern and engine room had been removed and replaced with the stern of a T-2 tanker—the kind built in abundance during World War II. This made her stern much higher than the original structure had been, and you could identify *Beechglen* from miles away it. In addition to being distinctive, the high stern was also a wind-catcher.

Beechglen was one of the last working lake freighters with "telescoping" hatch covers. Each hatch cover consisted of a series

165

of steel plates, or leaves that nested together when open and over-lapped when closed. Her 21 hatches were not watertight unless covered with tarps made specifically for that purpose. It was a big job to tarp her down after loading cargo and then closing the telescoping hatch covers, especially in the winter. The tarps were stiff and frozen with ice; the deckhands had to practically wrestle them into place to secure them. It was hard work. Still, year after year, the same crew returned to the ship with very few complaints. *Beechglen* was a good ship with a good crew.

Beechglen was powered by a 3500-horsepower steam turbine, but when in reverse, it only could provide 40 revolutions per minute. Most boats today have 60 revolutions or more. Because of the lack of stopping power, the captain had to watch the forward speed closely when entering a lock.

Trouble with the High Stern

One trip, we were outbound at DeTour Village, Michigan, heading for Goderich, Ontario, and southwest gales were forecast for Lake Huron. We progressed all night toward Goderich, and I hoped the wind would die down so I would not have too much trouble getting through the piers. Still, because of her high stern's tendency to catch the wind, I knew I would have my hands full.

I awoke the next morning to gray skies, and saw that the wind had dropped

Beechglen and her high stern; photo by Dick Metz

down to 30 knots (around 34 mph). Three miles off the Goderich piers, I adjusted course, keeping upwind for the piers. With her high stern, I had to keep her speed up so she would not set down on me. But I couldn't have too much speed so that I could stop her once inside the piers. At half speed and about half a mile from the piers, I gave the order to let go of the stern anchor. By doing that, I could turn the ship enough to get inside the harbor to unload the ship.

Once inside the piers, I rang up full astern in order to stop her forward motion so I could turn and go into the harbor. With only 40 revolutions astern, she was not stopping soon enough for me. There was a concrete wall ahead that was coming closer much faster than I wanted. Finally, the anchor found its mark, and the chain snapped out of the water with the sudden tension on it. The ship stopped with the bow only feet away from the concrete wall. I lost some more of my hair that day.

Full Reverse

On another occasion, I entered Lock 3 in the Welland Canal. We were empty except for ballast, so as soon as the bow entered the lock, I ordered the speed set at half astern to eat up some of her forward speed. I saw that she wasn't slowing as much as I wanted her to, so I rang up full astern to slow her some more. Then the wheelsman said, "Cap, they gave you full ahead!"

Crash

I looked up at the revolutions per minute meter, saw the ship was still going full ahead, and immediately rang up double full astern, but it was too late. By the time the engine room responded and I got the double full astern, *Beechglen's* bow hit the concrete sill—a ledge—at the edge of the lock.

I could hear bending of steel plates. She came to a shuddering stop. She hit the lock with such force that all the doors in my room flew open and shut all at the same time. We had to tie up above the lock for a Canadian Steamship Inspection.

This was the beginning of the end for the *Beechglen*. Her bow stem (the frontmost part of the ship) was pushed back, and most of the bow plates were buckled from the crash into the sill. Temporary repairs were made, and we finished out the year with her. In the end, she lay dormant in Owen Sound, Ontario, for a year before finally heading to the scrapyard.

Saying Goodbye

Eventually, the day came when two tugs were called to tow her to the scrapyard, just as had happened with her sister ships that had once sailed for the Soo River Company. I was on another ship and had just retired to my room after passing buoys 11 and 12 in southern Lake Huron, when I was called by the mate. "Cap, the *Beechglen* is being towed by two tugs."

I went back to the pilothouse to see her one last time. She did not display any navigation lights, but there was no mistaking that high stern as she passed in darkness. She was ready to go; it was time, and I was not sad to see her go.

The *Willowglen*; photo by Marc Dease

THE ANCHOR

Ship: *Willowglen*
Rank: Captain
Year: 1992

I took the exams to become a Captain in Thunder Bay, Ontario. (In the industry, it's called writing for your Master's certificate or ticket.) After passing all of the written tests, all that was left was the final oral exam, or "orals." During this exam, you come face-to-face with the examiner, and he tests you on your knowledge accumulated from your time at sea and from your years of study.

On my first day of orals, I walked into the examiner's office at 0800, dressed in a suit and tie. I spent 30 minutes sweating as I waited for the examiner. Finally, I was called into the exam room to meet "The Man." He, too, wore a suit and tie. After introductions, we sat down to begin the orals.

We took a short lunch break and were back at it again. He asked me questions and I answered as best as I could. By 1630, we both sat there exhausted, suit coats hanging over our chairs, open collars, and loose ties. We were both wringing wet, even though outside it was 15 degrees below zero that day.

In all, I went through three days of orals. At then end of each day, the dress was the same: coats on the chairs, open collars, ties off, and shirt sleeves rolled up.

"Let me have it," I thought. "After three days, what can he possibly ask me that I don't know?"

Wrong! The examiner looked me straight in the eyes and asked, "Mr. Metz, what, in your opinion, is one of the most important pieces of equipment aboard a ship?"

I took my time thinking about the answer, as it seemed really an easy question. I thought for a while and said to myself, "Radar," because I could plot the speed and course of ships close by, and radar was invaluable in fog. So, proudly, I answered, "Radar."

"Well, radar is very important," he replied, "but what else is just as important?"

Not radar, eh? Well, what else is on the bridge? "Okay, I got it this time," I thought.

"Okay, VHF marine radio," I said.

"Important, but guess again," he said.

Well, I had to really think about this, so again my mind went back to the wheelhouse, looking for something just as important as radar and radio. "Updated charts?" I said.

"Nope!"

My thinking cap was getting dull, so I tried, "A powerful engine with good back up."

"Nope!"

Well, I had had it. So before asking him what the correct answer was, I decided I was going to make a joke out of this mess. So I said, "The wheelhouse coffee pot."

"Mr. Metz, this is serious business! Anchors: the answer is a ship's anchors."

Anchors? I thought to myself, "The only time I ever used an anchor is when we had to go to anchor. No big deal."

Wrong! Man, was I wrong.

Lesson Learned

In September 1992, I was master of the *Willowglen*, and we had loaded a heavy cargo of iron ore in Quebec City to be discharged at Burns Harbor, Indiana. *Willowglen* was underpowered and was slow with a heavy load, especially against the St. Lawrence River current. Nevertheless, we had a good run all the way up the Seaway and through the Welland Canal.

We were cruising under the Mackinac Bridge when the Coast Guard posted northwest gale warnings for Lake Michigan. I ordered a course change to hug the eastern coast of Wisconsin for shelter, and I slowed down the ship. We estimated it'd take 26 hours to sail from the bridge to Burns Harbor, and the gale was expected to last at least 24 hours.

Burns Harbor is one port you don't want to try to make in a northerly gale, since that means the wind would be blowing parallel to the direction you're traveling, pushing against the entire length of the ship, and you might not make it through the piers.

The old girl made a good trip across the lake. When we passed Milwaukee, the wind was down to 30 knots (about 33 miles per hour), so we altered course for Burns Harbor.

One hour from the piers, I called our agent with our ETA. He said the MV *Stewart J. Cort* was a few hours behind us, also headed for Burns Harbor, and she would unload her cargo first. We agreed that *Willowglen* would go in first, start unloading, and then shift up to the end of the dock when the *Cort* arrived. The *Cort* would unload, and when they were finished, we would shift back and finish unloading.

We were three miles away and the wind was still out of the north when I began lining her up for the piers. I steered her into the wind and when close to the piers, I rang up full ahead to get her inside.

When the stern cleared the piers, I rang up full astern (reverse) and dropped the stern anchor. A mate was stationed on the stern to watch the anchor chain so it would not get caught in the propeller.

Inside the harbor, *Willowglen* finally stopped going ahead, so we backed up toward the anchor, and picked it up to stow it in its pocket. With the wind still out of the north, I could not line up to the dock right, so I dropped the port anchor, which swung the bow around just right, and I then raised the anchor. The wind was on my stern now and we were moving too fast to dock safely, so I had to drop the starboard anchor to slow her down and make the dock. By the time we were tied up, I was all "anchored out."

A few hours later, we had to move up the dock so the *Cort* could come in. I watched the big ship come through the piers, turn, come alongside the dock, stop, and "step" sideways where it nestled gently up against the dock. This was accomplished with great ease and in half the time it took me to make the same dock with a ship half the *Cort's* size.

I watched her depart the same way. Out through the piers she went. I couldn't help being a little jealous of the *Cort's* equipment, which included bow thrusters—propellers embedded in the front of a ship that help make it more maneuverable and an engine with "twin screws" (two propellers) instead of the *Willowglen's* one.

The *Willowglen*; photo by Marc Dease

"It must be nice to have all that, I thought." The *Cort's* anchors didn't have a scratch on them.

We finished unloading and had to stem the ship around off the dock. This meant that we had to push the front of the bow up against a steel plate on the dock, affix it with mooring cables, and then go slow ahead with the rudder turned hard to the left or the right. This would cause the stern to slowly swing around, and when it did, you let go of the mooring cables and back the ship out slowly. Then you turn the ship and go out through the harbor.

We started out. The wind was still from the north, and the stern would not come into the wind. So we dropped the starboard anchor, which helped us line up with the piers. We then pulled the anchor up and out into the lake we went.

173

About two hours out, our office called the *Willowglen* with a change of orders. We were to head for Thunder Bay to load instead of Goderich. The plan had been to refuel our thirsty fuel bunkers at Goderich. "I won't have enough fuel to get to Thunder Bay and then back down to the canal to refuel."

"Well, you'll have to find a place to get fuel," was the answer.

I called the agent in Chicago to tell him of my problem.

"I'll call you right back," he said.

Meanwhile, I called Thunder Bay and the Canadian Soo Locks, but there was no Bunker C (marine fuel) to be had in those ports.

The agent called back. "Turn around and head for Indiana Harbor," he said. "The harbor's full of ships, but the fuel barge can refuel you at anchor."

So that's what we did. Inside the harbor, we let the port anchor go. The barge came over and tied up alongside. After our welcome bunker fuel was aboard, we turned around by using a combination of the anchor and the engine.

When we were all lined up for the piers, we heaved up the hook and packed it away.

Out on Lake Michigan and on course for the Mackinac Bridge, I walked up to the bow, cup of coffee in hand, and looked at the anchor. It was so shiny from dropping it so many times that I think I saw my face in it.

And it turned out just how right my examiner was during those oral examinations. The anchor really is one of the most important pieces of equipment aboard a ship.

The *Oakglen*; photo by Todd Davidson

THE CADET

Ship: *Oakglen*
Rank: Captain
Year: 1982

In the 1970s, P&H Shipping Company was involved with a cadet program where a young man who was enrolled in the Owen Sound Marine School could go aboard one of their ships to learn firsthand knowledge about all phases of shipboard experience.

With this experience he could receive a third mate's license. I did not believe in the cadet program because I thought that to become a third mate you had to start from the ground and work your way up the ladder, like I did. I started as a deckhand and worked my way up learning all the jobs firsthand. The list included cleaning out cargo holds, drying them so you could load

175

another cargo, handling the mooring cables when tying up the ship, putting on hatches by running the hatch crane, and scraping off rust and then giving these spots a coat of primer paint and then a top coat. I started as deckhand in 1964, and it took me until 1973 to get my third mate's license. I figured you must know these jobs in order to give orders to a crew.

The Oakglen; photo by James Hoffman

We had a young lad just out of marine school come aboard as a cadet. He was from abroad and couldn't speak English well. We couldn't pronounce his name but called him Zoakie, which was okay with him. Our cadet expected to wear his white shirt and stay in the wheelhouse all the time. As time went on I noticed that every time I entered the pilothouse he was either standing in front of the radar or sitting on my chair.

The first and last thing I did as I entered the bridge was look into the radar to see if any traffic was near and to check our position. I always had to say 'excuse me' before I could look into the radar or 'excuse me, you're sitting on my chair.' One night I was called to the bridge because a ship was on a collision course with ours. The mate on watch said he tried calling the other ship but got no answer, so he called me. The ship was rolling with reduced visibility, and as I entered the pilothouse I immediately went to the radar to see the other ship bearing down on us. And there was our cadet standing at the radar. I had no time to say 'excuse me,' so I bumped him aside and took control of the situation.

This happened more and more, and finally I told him, "When you hear me coming up the stairs, you leave the bridge and go into the chart room. If you do not like that, then you are to leave the pilothouse immediately." I also told him to never sit in the captain's chair again.

The mates were more patient with our cadet than I was, and they taught him how to receive the MAFOR (weather reports), check the water temperature and weather-related reports, how to check the ship's position, not to mention how to make a good pot of coffee, etc.

When we were at an unloading port, our cadet was again standing in the wheelhouse wearing his white shirt. So while we were unloading our cargo of grain, I asked the cadet if he wanted to become a good third mate, and he said, "Yes."

I asked, "Well, how are you going to become a good third mate by standing in the wheelhouse?" I then told him a good mate had to know his job in order to give orders to his men. I told him to see the mate and get a pair of blue coveralls, a yellow hard hat and gloves and get down into the cargo hold and start cleaning it. I told him that he must work with the deckhands for four hours a day and do what they do.

I said, "You must start from the bottom and work your way up the ladder."

Our cadet did not like that, and he called the company. They said, "He is the captain."

So we had our cadet aboard for the summer, and he worked with the deckhands four hours a day. He got out of my way when I entered the wheelhouse, and we all got along just fine. When I signed him off and he went back to school, he thanked me for all the experience he gained. I told him that he would make a fine third mate some day.

Captain Metz with a bell awarded to him for being the first laker into port; photo by Dick Metz

FIRST IN PORT, TWICE IN A YEAR

Ship: *Mapleglen*
Rank: Captain
Year: 1999

In March 1999, we fitted out the *Mapleglen* in Owen Sound, Ontario. After completing our inspection, we departed for Thunder Bay to load our first load of the new season. It was grain, and half would be discharged at the ADM terminal in Windsor, Ontario, and the rest of the cargo at Goderich.

It had been a mild winter, and ice conditions were very good. There was very little ice in the St. Marys River, and Lake Superior was wide-open all the way to Thunder Bay. We made very good time.

Lake Shippers called me for an updated ETA, and I was told that we would be the first ship into Thunder Bay for the 1999 navigation season.

For years, certain ports around the Great Lakes have celebrated the first ship to arrive. There are usually festivities in honor of her captain and crew, and ships often raced each other just to win the title of "First Ship." The captain usually received a traditional silk top hat and was usually wined and dined.

Over the years, such celebrations have become less elaborate, and some have fallen by the wayside. But some ports still practiced the tradition, and Thunder Bay was one of them

Of all the years I'd been on the lakes, it was the first time I'd been on the first ship. I didn't know what to expect, so the mate had the deckhands clean up the ship. When we arrived in port, we had all the flags flying and made a short tour around the harbor. Then we tied up at Elevator Pool #1.

1st Vessel - 1999 Season

MV Maplegl

Captain Richard Metz

Owned by P & H Shipping

20, 000 tonnes of canola

Arrival - March 27th   Departure - March 2

photo by Dick Metz

An award given to Metz and the crew for arriving first;

Our representative at the company (P&H) in Thunder Bay called. "I'll pick you up around noon for a quick luncheon," he said.

"Is this going to be big affair?" I asked.

"No, just a few elevator employees out for lunch."

I felt good about that, since I'm not much for formality.

Then he added, "Oh, yes, wear your uniform."

A small lunch with the boys, and I had to wear a full-dress uniform? Something didn't make sense.

The Big Show

I had just finished dressing when my phone rang. It was the first mate, Kent Powell, informing me that the press was aboard and wanted to see me. We all met in the wheelhouse. The mayor of Thunder Bay was there along with the city fathers, bigwigs from the grain elevators, a TV crew, plus a reporter from CKPR radio and one from the local newspaper. And I had been told this was not going to be a big deal!

First Mate Kent had a smirk on his face; he knew I was not into publicity like this. Most of the crew made jokes about me being like a fish out of water, and that this was the first time they'd ever seen the Old Man in uniform.

"Watch how this is done," I told Kent. "When you become captain, you'll know what to do." I left him with a smirk on my face.

The whole event was like something out of Hollywood with all the lights and sound equipment and people running around. Then came my rehearsal. I was told where to stand and what questions I was to be asked. I took off my white hat to try on the traditional silk top hat. It was too small for my head, so I removed the hat and handed it back to the mayor. He whispered into my ear, "You can't keep the hat. I must take it back after the ceremony."

I whispered back, "That's okay, Mayor, it doesn't fit anyhow!"

While the television camera rolled, I gave a brief description of our trip to Thunder Bay and a small, unrehearsed speech about being the first ship into the port. Then the mayor handed me the silk top hat and, after a short speech, shook my hand. When the camera stopped, he asked for the hat back. I gave it back, and they all left the ship as fast as they had come aboard.

At noon, the P&H representative's car arrived, and we left for the luncheon. It was at the Airline Motor Lounge. As we entered, a young man walked up. "Are you looking for the navigation party?" he asked.

"Well, not a party, just a small lunch get-together."

He showed us the door to a large room. I took a peek inside, and it was filled with people. "This can't be the room," I said. "There are too many people here."

"That's the room you're looking for," the young man said.

There must have been 200 people sitting at tables. As we walked in, the loudspeaker blasted. "Ladies and gentlemen, may I have your attention! Captain Metz from *Mapleglen* just arrived, the first ship to arrive in Thunder Bay to open the 1999 navigation season."

The audience stood up and applauded. "Congratulations!" they all said. Flash bulbs exploded all around me. I was in shock. The mass of people's faces went blank before my eyes. Never before had I been a guest of honor.

I received a special plaque with my name and the name of the ship with the date and a nice painting of a lake schooner sailing in Thunder Bay Harbor with the Sleeping Giant in the background. Each of the crew received a white ball cap printed with the Thunder Bay logo. I enjoyed everything, plus some nice gifts, but was glad when the ship was loaded and we left for Windsor.

First, Again!

In more than 30 years, I'd never been first in a port, but that year it happened not once, but twice. I was also the first ship into Windsor, Ontario. Two "firsts" in the same year!

When ADM phoned the ship to say we would be the first into that port, I couldn't believe what I heard. "Do you have a uniform?" they asked. "Have all of your flags flying. The press will be aboard as soon as you dock."

Here we go again. Kent was smirking again.

The same type of ceremony took place in Windsor with television cameras and newspaper reporters. This time, I was presented a large brass bell with an inscription that read: "Port of Windsor, S/S *Mapleglen* Commanded by Captain Richard Metz, First Laker, March 31, 1999, The Windsor Harbour Commission."

I told the mayor about the silk top hat affair in Thunder Bay and how they had taken the hat back after the ceremony. She said, "We won't take the bell back. You can keep it."

All in all, this was quite an honor for me to have two "firsts," especially since this would be my final year as master of a Great Lakes vessel. I would retire in five months.

Captain Metz and the ceremonial top hat; photo by Dick Metz

The *Mapleglen*; photo courtesy of www.boatnerd.com

TIME TO LET GO THE ANCHOR

Ship: *Mapleglen*
Rank: Captain
Year: 1999

Eventually, I found myself thinking how nice it would be to stay home and enjoy my Florida home, fly my airplane, vacation with my wife, work around the house, and never have to pack my suitcase again. But when would I know that I wanted to retire?

In fact, the question had occasionally been on mind for the last couple years. One day, I was talking to a retired captain, and I asked him my burning question, "When will I know?"

"Someday it will hit you, and you will know it's time to retire," he said.

The old skipper was right. That day came, and it did hit me. I felt it when my wife drove me to the Orlando airport for my next 35-day stint on the *Mapleglen*. I sat waiting for my flight that was two hours late, and the feeling got stronger.

Finally, while in the air heading for Toronto, the lady in the seat in front of me tried to recline the back of her seat. It hit my knees, and she gave me an unpleasant look. The feeling got stronger yet.

Because of bad weather, the plane had to go into a holding pattern until it was safe to land, another hour late. When I walked up to the limousine company's desk, the attendant said it had left, and I had to wait three more hours for the next one to arrive.

I was joining the ship in the Welland Canal, just a 20-minute ride from Buffalo, but the company insisted on flying me all the way over to Toronto, then cabbing it back to the canal, which, to me, did not make any sense at all. I had actually flown right over the ship on the way to Toronto.

After a long wait, the limo arrived, and after another three-hour ride, I got to the canal and went aboard my ship.

Then it hit me. "That is it. I am going to retire." So I called my wife in Florida and told her how I felt.

She said, "Good. Come on home."

I called the company and told them this would be the last for me, and when my 35 days were up, I was going to retire.

I started training First Mate Kent Powell on shiphandling, showing him how to anchor a ship and how to make all the walls at all the locks from Thunder Bay to Montreal.

To be a good ship handler, it was necessary to have a certain knack for it.

I knew skippers just didn't have the knack for shiphandling; I don't think one can easily learn it. You either you have it or you don't. My first observations of Kent's shiphandling abilities told me immediately that he had the knack. Kent was an intelligent young man, and he reminded me of myself when I first started out sailing. I was so sure of Kent's ability to handle a ship the right way that I would not come up on the bridge to watch him make a wall or progress through of the locks.

Then I called P&H to inform them that Kent was ready to sail his own ship.

In August 1999, I was called to the bridge of the *Mapleglen* for the last time. We were six miles from the piers at Port Weller, Ontario. I looked in my mirror to check the four gold bars on each shoulder and make sure I was dressed just right as I walked up to the bridge.

I took over the con (command of the ship) from the mate, and at Call In Point 15, I called Seaway Welland with my position. I was given the okay to enter Lock 1 and told to make a security call (a radio call) once at the piers.

A fine-looking vessel; photo by Rob Farrow

I made Lock 1, and before Lock 2, I called Kent to the bridge. He made the lock while I went down to my quarters to change out of my uniform. I removed my gold bars and put them together.

When we were secured in Lock 3, I went back to the bridge and handed Kent, the new master, my gold bars. "They've brought me good luck all these years, and I wish you the same luck." We shook hands, and he thanked me for everything.

I walked down the deck, shaking hands with most of the crew. My taxi was waiting at Lock 3 to take me to Buffalo, from where I would fly to Florida. I felt good and wanted to go.

I walked down the gangplank onto the lock wall and started toward the taxi. Captain Powell blew me a master's salute—three long, two short—from the ship's whistle. I froze for a moment, then turned toward the pilothouse and saluted, turned again and walked to the cab. That salute was an honor for me. What a beautiful send-off. Thank you, Captain Powell. I guess something must have flown into my eyes, because they were watering.

The Mapleglen and Oakglen waiting for the scrapyard; photo courtesy of Kent Maylo

GLOSSARY

ABEAM: at a right angle to the length of a ship; parallel to it

ABLE SEAMAN: a sailor with at least 12 months of experience on the water who then passes the able seaman examination (or in marine parlance, "writes for the AB ticket")

BOSUN'S CHAIR: a harness-like device that crewmembers use to get from the deck of the ship to the ground at locks, piers and so on

DECKHAND: a low-ranking crew member who helps tie up the ship at locks and harbors, attaches/removes hatch covers and cleans/washes the deck/ship

DECKWATCH: the crewmember responsible for overseeing the deckhands, including waking up the crew

DOWNBOUND: heading "down" the Great Lakes (away from Lake Superior) and toward the Atlantic

ENGINE ROOM: the ship department required for maintaining and repairing the ship's engine and generators

FOGHORN: loud horns that ships must sound during foggy periods; they help prevent collisions

FOLLOWING SEA: waves that are traveling in the same direction as the boat

GALE: a storm that produces winds ranging from 39 miles per hour to 54 miles per hour; gales are common in November, when the relatively warm waters of the Great Lakes interact with cold air pushed south from Canada

GREENHORN: a crewmember who is brand new to the shipping industry; a rookie

GYROCOMPASS: a compass that uses a rotating gyroscope instead of a magnet to indicate direction

HEAD SEA: waves that are traveling directly against a vessel's course

HOOK: slang for the anchor

IRON MIKE: slang for a ship's autopilot

LAKE CARRIERS' ASSOCIATION: A group representing the U.S.-owned shipping companies on the Great Lakes; the Canadian counterpart is the Canadian Shipowners Association

LAYUP: the period when a ship is in port for refurbishment or repair; economic conditions can also cause ships to be laid up for long periods if it's not profitable to operate them

LIFEBOAT TICKET: A U.S. Coast Guard certification that a sailor knows how to launch and operate a life boat

LOCK: an engineering device that helps ships—even those hundreds of feet long—move between two different bodies of water that have differing elevations; a ship usually enters a lock, ties up, and a gate closes behind the ship; the water level is either raised or lowered, and when the ship is at the same level as the next body of water, the gate is opened and the ship goes on its way

MAFOR: a marine weather forecast broadcast in code

MATE: a licensed member of the deck crew

MESS: the galley area, where food is served

MONKEY ISLAND: a raised platform that is one step above the pilothouse's deck

NOR'EASTER: a large storm that forms in the Atlantic and features winds that blow from the northeast to the southwest; they often produce copious amounts of snow

OILSKINS: foul-weather gear; sailors once wore oil-treated clothing, which served to waterproof the gear; today, more contemporary waterproofing methods are used

PILOT: a temporary member of the crew who joins the ship if the captain/crew are not licensed to sail in those waters; a pilot's job is to know the specific waters in which they are sailing, including all of its hazards and quirks

PILOTHOUSE: the area on the bridge where the ship is navigated

PORT: the nautical term for left

QUARTERING SEA: waves that are arriving at about a 45 degree angle to a ship's heading

RDF: radio direction finder; a now antiquated system that enabled sailors to find the direction/bearing to fixed radio sources, enabling them to locate their position

RELIEF CAPTAIN: a captain who fills in for other captains when they go on vacation, are injured, etc.

SOOGIE: scrubbing down the ship—a job done by deckhands

STAND BY: a term meaning, "wait at the ready"

STARBOARD: the nautical term for right

STORM: a weather system even stronger than a gale; its winds range from 55 miles per hour and higher; in extreme circumstances, winds can even exceed 75 miles per hour

TICKET: a Coast Guard certificate

UPBOUND: heading "up" the Great Lakes (toward Lake Superior) and away from the Atlantic

WHEELHOUSE: the area on the bridge where the ship is navigated (and where you'll find the wheel)

NAUTICAL DIRECTIONS

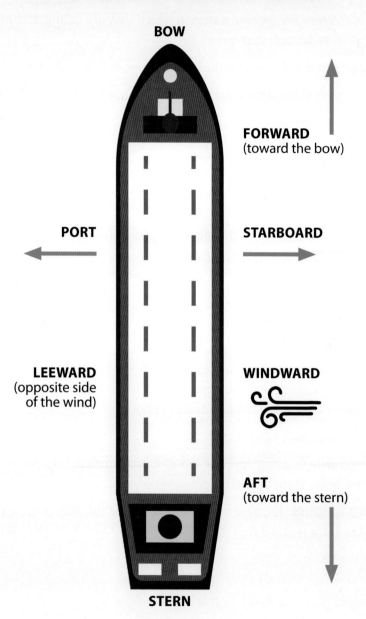

BOW

FORWARD
(toward the bow)

PORT

STARBOARD

LEEWARD
(opposite side
of the wind)

WINDWARD

AFT
(toward the stern)

STERN

ASK THE CAPTAIN

You grew up in Wisconsin, near Rhinelander, which is 70-some-miles from the Great Lakes. What drew you to the Inland Seas?

Captain Metz: When I was young, my Dad lived in Canada, and I was talking to him and asked, "Where is Canada?" Right across the lake he said. So, he drove me to Ontonogan, Michigan, and I could not get over how big that lake was and how beautiful it was. Ever since the day I got my first car, I'd drive up to see the lake. I had a sleeping bag and spent the nights and days looking at the lake. And I still do it to this day.

When you first encountered the 620-foot-long Thomas Wilson, *you describe it as a jaw-dropping experience. Today, most ships on the lakes are much larger, sometimes almost twice the* Wilson's *size. What was it like seeing that change, and how did it impact your job as captain? How much different is handling a 600-footer like the* Wilson *than a 700-footer like the* Mapleglen?

Captain Metz: I like the bigger ships, as the quarters were newer and bigger. I used to go up to the pilothouse and pull up a chair to the front window and get used to her size. All ships act the same, the difference was you had to get used to the size, and it took longer to handle a long and wider ship.

When you began your career on the lakes, shipwrecks occurred with some frequency. The Cedarville *went down after a collision the year after you joined the* Wilson's *crew, and the* Daniel J. Morrell, *the year after that. Today, while absolutely still possible, shipwrecks are much rarer, and a bulk carrier hasn't gone down since the* Edmund Fitzgerald *in 1975. What, in your view, has caused that change? Do you think another will happen on the lakes in the future?*

Captain Metz: What caused the change is better weather forecasting—at a touch of a button you can get a up to date weather 24 hours a day. We also have better and stronger-built ships; years ago they used rivets, and today they weld ship hulls. We also have better, up-to-date navigation systems, including radar, GPS and AIS, not to mention bow thrusters, and more powerful diesel engines. And, yes, there will always be sinking of ships. Look at the *Titanic*!

Your father was a resident of Canada, and you had Landed Immigrant Status (equivalent to a U.S. Green Card), so you've sailed in both the American fleet and the Canadian fleet. How are the Canadian fleet and the American fleets different?

Captain Metz: There was little difference between the two countries. Most of the older ships that I sailed once belonged to the US. Same cargoes, same ports, same bodies of water. But the flag was different!

When you started out on the Lakes in 1964, the Space Age was just beginning; weather satellites were in their infancy and forecasts were much less reliable. Describe the differences that technology has played on the lakes, especially pertaining to the weather, and the decision-making process of whether or not to seek shelter.

Captain Metz: The difference is years ago we could only receive the weather reports at 0600 and at 1800 hours per day, from just two stations at Duluth, Minnesota and Lorain, Ohio. Now there are weather reports 24 hours a day. Ship-to-shore radio stations were also bad at mid-lake on Lake Superior; you couldn't reach a shore radio station, especially in bad weather. At the time, we had only AM radios, now it is all FM. Our old radars use to make one sweep or scan every three minutes; today they scan 32 times per minute, and the radars are more powerful and include a lot more options, not to mention other tools such as GPS, electric charts, and AIS.

Did you know anyone on the Edmund Fitzgerald *or the subsequent search for her?*

Captain Metz: No, I did not know any of her crew. I heard the skipper of the *Anderson* talking to the USCG that night and also heard the announcement that she had gone down. All night long I heard the USCG calling the *Fitzgerald* over and over. I was at anchor in Thunder Bay Harbor that night along with other ships.

You were active during the decline of the U.S. steel industry, which directly impacted the shipping industry; during your career, many ships were laid up, then scrapped, and at the same time, vessels also became more efficient, and crew sizes diminished, especially with the introduction of the newer tug-barge combinations. How would you describe the atmosphere of the industry over time?

Captain Metz: At one time I use to see many ships on the lakes, and when we got to the Soo Locks, it was a very busy place. We had to check our speed, go to anchor and even tie up to wait our turn to be lock through. As the years went by, there were fewer ships and less traffic at the locks and in the rivers, on the Welland Canal and the Seaway. My last years of sailing I could make the Welland Canal in 10 to 12 hours instead of 24 hours; at the Soo we very seldom met a ship, and the locks were open all of the time.

Do you think contemporary crews rely too heavily on modern technology?

Captain Metz: No, I do not think that. Technology is a great, and we have to have it to make navigation safe. Even with all the technology we have today ships still run aground, like the

M/V *Roger Blough*, which ran aground last fall. That grounding cost the owners $4.5 million.

You were a wreck diver, and you've dived on some of the more famous/impressive wrecks out there, especially those near Isle Royale. What attracted you to wreck diving?

Captain Metz: I was always interested what was on the bottom of a lake. I visited a dive shop in Superior, Wisconsin, and they were getting ready to go on a diving trip to Isle Royale to dive on the shipwreck *America*. I asked the lead diver what it was like diving on a shipwreck, he told me, and I was hooked.

You were also a tugboat captain when you worked at Isle Royale National Park. What drew you there? Did you have any run-ins with wildlife (moose/wolves) in your time there?

Captain Metz: I started diving on Isle Royale shipwreck, and there were a lot of wrecks around the island. It is such a beautiful place. No, I never hard a wolf howl, and I never saw one there. I did see a lot of moose; I had a tame cow and I used to feed her a head of cabbage from my porch. I was also chased by a young bull at Mott Island; when I got off my tugboat, I ran to the nearest house.

You're also an airplane pilot. When did you get your license? What kind of planes do you fly? Do you still fly today?

Captain Metz: I received my Singe Engine, Land Certification in 1981 and bought a Cessna 172, 1976 Sky Hawk before I got my license to fly. I sold my plane six years ago and have not flown since.

What were your favorite ships that you sailed on? Your least favorite? Do you have any favorites that are still on the lakes today? What do you think of the 1000-footers? The new tug-barge combinations?

Captain Metz: I had several favorite ships that I sailed. The *Soo River Trader* was the best-looking ship, The *Mapleglen* had very nice quarters and a bow thruster, and the *Oakglen* (2) was a fast ship and very powerful. The old steamers were beautiful-looking ships and had a nice rake to them and all were classic-looking Great Lakes ships. The 1000-footers of today are basically an engine pushing a barge; they have no looks at all, and all of them look the same.

I've read that some shipping companies are experimenting with self-navigating ships, akin to the self-driving cars now on the road in certain cities. Do you foresee automation becoming a concern for those on the lakes? Could an automation system replace a human crew?

Captain Metz: Yes, I foresee someday the ships will not have any crews aboard; today, there are cars with no drivers, planes that can land themselves. When I first started sailing, we had a crew of 34 men, now it is down to 12 and some even less.

Do you miss the Great Lakes?

Captain Metz: I live on Lake Superior, and I watch the ships sailing upbound and downbound only three miles off. I have a marine radio, and if I know a ship I will call them. I say it's Captain Metz but nobody remembers me, as I have been retired for 17 years. I do not miss sailing the Great Lakes.

CAPTAIN METZ'S SHIPS

Thomas Wilson
Built: 1941
Length: 620 feet
Cargo: Iron Ore
Fate: Scrapped in 1987, it sank on the way to the scrapyard in Taiwan

B. F. Jones
Built: 1907
Length: 520 feet
Cargo: Iron Ore
Fate: Scrapped in Spain in 1973

J. E. Colombe
Built: 1953
Length: 45 feet
Cargo: Responsible for towing barges full of supplies for Isle Royale National Park
Fate: Still in service

John Dykstra
Built: 1953
Length: 644 feet
Cargo: Iron Ore
Fate: Scrapped in 1987

Georgian Bay
Built: 1953
Length: 620 feet
Cargo: Grain, other bulk cargoes
Fate: Scrapped in 1989

Incan Superior
Built: 1974
Length: 373 feet
Cargo: Train cars filled with newsprint
Fate: Still in service, but in British Columbia

H. C. Heimbecker
Built: 1905
Length: 569 feet
Cargo: Grain, other bulk cargoes
Fate: Scrapped in 1981

Soo River Trader
Built: 1906
Length: 530 feet
Cargo: Grain, other bulk cargoes
Fate: Scrapped in 1984

Judith M. Pierson
Built: 1917
Length: 550 feet
Cargo: Grain, other bulk cargoes
Fate: Scrapped in 1984

Oakglen
Built: 1953
Length: 714 feet
Cargo: Grain, other bulk cargoes
Fate: Scrapped in 2004

Willowglen
Built: 1943
Length: 620 feet
Cargo: Iron ore, grain and other bulk cargoes
Fate: First docked as a grain storage barge, then scrapped in 2005 at Alang, India.

Mapleglen
Built: 1960
Length: 715 feet
Cargo: Iron ore, grain and other bulk cargoes
Fate: Scrapped in 2003

Beechglen
Built: 1923
Length: 586 feet
Cargo: Iron ore, grain and other bulk cargoes
Fate: Scrapped in 1994

RANKS ABOARD GREAT LAKES VESSELS

DECKHANDS

Captain (requires master's license)

First Mate (requires mate's license)

Second Mate (requires mate's license)

Third Mate (requires mate's license)

Wheelsman (requires Able Seaman certificate)

Able Seaman (requires Able Seaman certificate)

Deckwatch (unlicensed)

Deckhand (unlicensed)

ENGINE ROOM

Chief Engineer (requires engineer's license)

First assistant engineer (requires engineer's license)

Second assistant engineer (requires engineer's license)

Third assistant engineer (requires engineer's license)

Motorman (unlicensed)

Oiler (unlicensed)

Wiper (unlicensed)

GALLEY

Cook/steward (unlicensed)

ABOUT THE AUTHOR

After only ten years driving truck, he was drawn to the Great Lakes. He had always enjoyed watching the boats and ships moving seemingly effortlessly on the water going places he could only dream.

With very little encouragement, Capt. Metz decided to try for a job working on the Great Lakes ships. He started working on the boats in 1964 as a deckhand. He knew right away that life aboard a laker was what he wanted to do all the rest of his life. He worked his way through the ranks to become a Great Lakes Sea Captain in 1980.

Captain Metz enjoyed every minute of his career and continues to enjoy remembering and writing about his life on the lakes, even today. In 2003, Captain R. Metz wrote his first book, *Sea Stories*. That book talked about his experiences in a clear and conversational manner offering his fascinating insight into the world of Great Lakes shipping. Capt. Metz's second book, *Life Aboard a Laker from 1964 to 1999*, followed in this same vein, detailing the start of his career through his different positions on lakers, his studies, and what his choice of career meant to him. This book expands on Capt. Metz's previous work, and includes additional stories, full-color photos, and a question-and-answer session with Captain Metz.